The Unofficial
ḤOBBIT
ḤANDBOOK

Dedication

Peter

For Mark Sehestedt, who has lived his life on the shores of Middle-earth.

Scott

For Heather and Socktopus with all my love.

Jeff

To everyone who finds in Middle-earth a bit of inspiration for living in *our* earth.

Acknowledgments

Peter

Thanks to my wife, who threatened physical violence unless I finished my part of the book. Thanks also to Rachel Scheller, who was, as an editor, far more patient with me than I would have been.

Scott

I'd like to thank my fellow Shire collective members Jeff, Ben and Peter for being great guys to work with. Also, thanks to Phil Sexton for helping brainstorm this whole idea. And many thanks to Claudean Wheeler, Rachel Scheller, and Kim Catanzarite for whipping this thing into shape in the eleventh hour.

Jeff

Thanks to Scott Francis for convincing me I really could offer something of value to this volume.

About the Shire Collective

Peter Archer is an editor at Adams Media in Avon, Massachusetts. He read Tolkien's works as a boy and continues to re-read *The Lord of the Rings* every few years so the magic will never fade. He lives in a converted parsonage on the south coast of Massachusetts with his wife and two decorative but essentially useless cats.

Scott Francis is a lifelong fanboy who loves all things sci-fi and fantasy. He is an editor for HOW Books, the author of *The Monster Spotter's Guide to North America*, and co-author of *The Writer's Book of Matches*.

Jeff Gerke is an editor and author of fiction and nonfiction including such books as the *Operation: Firebrand* novels and *Plot Versus Character: A Balanced Approach to Writing Great Fiction*. He is the founder and publisher of Marcher Lord Press, an indie press producing original science fiction and fantasy with a spiritual edge.

Table of Contents

Introduction

In the times before the race of men, the elves and wizards ruled. Great wars fought between the forces of good and evil shaped the future of things. Evil nearly triumphed, as evil often does, but for the deeds of a few small, courageous creatures known as hobbits.

The hobbits of JRR Tolkien's Middle-earth are simple folk, accustomed to living routine lives and enjoying simple pleasures. Their home—the Shire—is a place where everyone knows everyone, where a good day's work (or a good day's play) is held in high regard, and where good food, good drink, and good friends are all the riches anyone needs.

Most hobbits are content with their simple lives and rarely seek anything resembling adventure or mischief. But when danger finds its way to their doorstep, or adventure sweeps them up and takes them along its path (as danger and adventure sometimes do), hobbits can summon courage disproportionate to their small stature. Their loyalty and devotion to friends is unwavering. Their sense of right and wrong is unquestionable. They are, quite simply, good and honest folk.

In the age of man, we could stand to learn a thing or two from such creatures. Our world is complicated. It is overrun with politics, violence, corruption, and greed. We are obsessed with money and possessions. We are selfish, too rarely taking time to spend with our family, friends, and neighbors. We are constantly hurried and rush here and there, filling our bodies with fast food instead of taking time to enjoy a finely prepared meal. At the root of these things are the same evils that corrupted Middle-earth and threatened the hobbits and their simple way of life: selfishness, sloth, thirst for power, and greed.

In writing *The Hobbit* and *The Lord of the Rings*, Tolkien wasn't just telling an epic story about a mystical realm filled with fantastic creatures. He was creating a timeless parable that we can use to remind ourselves of the way a good and virtuous life should be lived. The hobbits, with their good-natured, trusting, and loyal personalities, represent the good qualities that people can aspire to.

Within the following pages, we'll examine the lives of hobbits and the lessons they impart. After all, who hasn't encountered a few "trolls" in their daily lives? Who hasn't had to outsmart a slimy creature obsessed with riches and power? Who hasn't had to summon the courage to face evil when they'd really rather sit down to a piping hot breakfast?

In one way or another we all have our own quests, our own burdens to carry, our own monsters to face—our own adventures. We may not be fighting actual dragons, but it can often seem like we are, and when you get right down to it, evil is evil, whatever form it may take. So be inspired by the little folk of the Shire and find your own way to be simple, good, and true ... just like a hobbit.

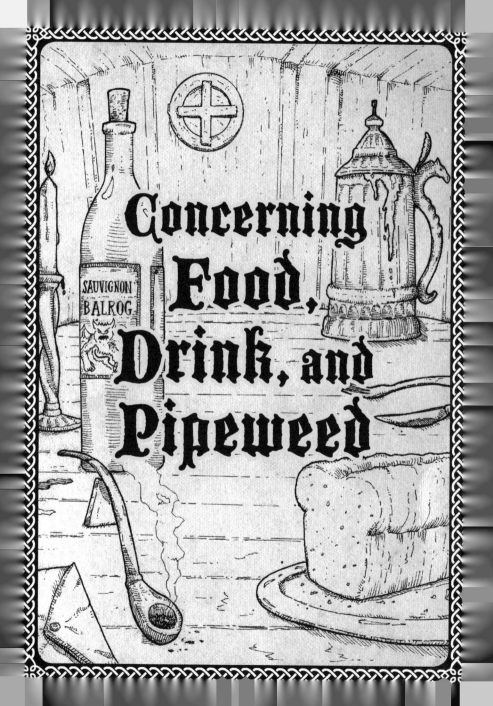

Concerning Food, Drink, and Pipeweed

There was hot soup, cold meats, a blackberry tart, new loaves, slabs of butter, and half a ripe cheese: good plain food, as good as the Shire could show, and homelike enough to dispel the last of Sam's misgivings (already much relieved by the excellence of the beer).

—From JRR Tolkien's *The Fellowship of the Ring*

If there's one thing hobbits are experts on, it's food and drink. Not fancy food and drink, mind you, because hobbits like good plain food—but plenty of it. Many of the rooms branching out from Bag End's central passageway are larders, and both Bilbo and later Frodo kept them well stocked. After receiving the Unexpected Party, which saw thirteen dwarves and one wizard sitting in his front parlor waiting for dinner to be served, Bilbo was always on the alert for guests. Frodo, having his own circle of friends, knew from experience that a lot of food is necessary in order to be considered a polite host.

However, hobbits aren't the only creatures in Middle-earth concerned with food and drink. Long, rich traditions exist among dwarves, elves, men, and even other creatures (Ents, for instance, know a thing or two about drinks). Let's consider some elements of this rich culinary tradition and what lessons they may hold for adventurers and travelers.

Hobbits

As earlier mentioned, hobbits eschew fancy foods prepared in rich sauces with exotic garnishes. They like plain food, and they serve it warm from the oven.

Meats

Hobbits raise pigs, cows, and sheep, but cattle are more often used for milk and sheep for wool than as meat sources. However, it's by no means unusual for hobbits to sit down to a hearty meal of roast beef, stewed to perfection with some herbs, salt, and potatoes. Roast mutton, too, makes a regular appearance in hobbit households, as well as bacon and sausages. There's a brief mention of cold chicken in *The Hobbit*, and hobbits are fond of eggs, so there must be chickens somewhere.

Two things that are off the hobbit diet are lamb and veal, so if you stop by the Floating Log or the Green Dragon for some evening sustenance, don't expect to see those dishes on the menu.

Hobbits are experienced hunters; many are capable with bows, and just about any hobbit has skill throwing rocks (and darts and quoits and anything else that requires some skill to throw). The result is that hobbits are well supplied with game, including deer, pheasant, pigeon, boar (rather rare in the Shire), and fox (lean, and not especially good to eat, but palatable in a period of famine).

Dried Meat

Hobbits are skilled at all sorts of meat preparation, including drying meat into jerky as provender for journeys. They don't make jerky a lot, since hobbits don't take journeys all that much, but every now and then when some adventurous party of halflings takes it into their heads to ride out to Bree for a couple of nights, it's handy to take along a few strips of dried meat.

Hobbits also know how to dry fruits for journeys and how to preserve them (see the next page).

Vegetables

In our world, the closest cousins to hobbits are Englishmen from the 1930s and 1940s. Therefore, it's a given that all hobbit vegetables are cooked only one way: boiled to extinction. It's a pity, really, because hobbits are expert gardeners and grow wonderful, flavorful produce. However, they are wont to toss shelled peas into a pot of boiling water, add a pinch of salt, and leave them to boil for half an hour. The resulting dull, gray mass can be shoveled down a hobbit's well-muscled throat in vast quantities.

Cheese

Hobbits are expert cheese makers, and in most hobbit holes, as well as inns along the Road, the weary traveler can find everything from bleu cheese to ripe cheddar. Cheese is usually served with the main meal, not as a separate dish, and can be taken on long journeys, as long as it is left in its rind and wrapped in leaves to keep it from drying out. Hobbits have been known to add such ingredients to their cheeses as beer, horseradish, and port wine, but as a rule they prefer simple cheeses to more complex ones.

Fruits

Hobbits adore fruit, both raw and cooked. In the year 1420, after the scouring of the Shire to remove the servants of the wizard Saruman, hobbit children "sat on the lawns under the plum-trees and ate, until they had made piles of stones like small pyramids or the heaped skulls of a conqueror, and then they moved on." A strange, ghastly image to accompany gluttony, but there you are.

In addition to gorging themselves on plums, apricots, apples, pears, and peaches, hobbits enjoy strawberries in cream, blueberries, blackberries, and raspberries, as well as rare fruits such as quince and persimmons that are scarcely found elsewhere in Middle-earth. Hobbits are adept at baking, creating an array of pies, tarts, scones, and fruit-laden biscuits. Fruit is also the basis of some hobbit wines and liqueurs.

Fruit is an essential part of the supplies of any traveler, and there are no better apples than those found in the orchards of the Shire.

Mushrooms

These are the quintessential hobbit food; as a lad, Frodo Baggins ranges over the Shire in search of them, venturing onto the lands of Farmer Maggot, with dismal consequences (for Frodo, that is). Mushrooms come in many varieties, and hobbits learn at an early age to distinguish between those that are good to eat and those best left alone. They can be cooked into such concoctions as mushroom and bacon pie (enough to feed a farmhouse full of hungry hobbits, and that's really saying something) and baked mushroom tart. Hobbits have even been known to eat them raw or with a little butter.

Butter, Cream, Jam, and Milk

Speaking of butter, churns are always busy around the Shire, turning out butter and cream. Butter can be wrapped in leaves and stored in a cool place, but it must be used relatively quickly. For this reason, the traveler is advised to forgo butter on his or her bread and to be contented with jam made from berries or quince.

There's plenty of milk, but alas, like butter, it spoils easily and should be drunk soon after it's produced. For the traveler, stick to ale or wine—or water, in a pinch.

Baking and Pickling

Hobbits bake constantly; this is necessary, given how much they eat. Bilbo was an experienced baker who produced tarts, pies (both meat and fruit varieties), and cakes (especially seed-cake). Some bakers among hobbits produce their wares for inns, but most hobbits bake what's necessary for their home consumption. Consequently, many fields of wheat and corn flourish throughout the Shire, and the miller of Hobbiton is a significant personage in the community.

Like all communities not possessed of refrigeration, the hobbits of the Shire are skilled at pickling and preserving in heavy stone crocks. They pickle not only cucumbers but vegetables of all kinds, including tomatoes, onions, beans, and beets.

What to Expect if You Invite a Hobbit to Dinner

Don't plan on having leftovers. Hobbits will eat until there's nothing left. They sail through the main meal, polish off dessert, and sit back for coffee and after-dinner drinks while "filling up the corners" with any odd scraps and bits of food within reach. Hobbits aren't picky about food, so long as there's plenty of it and it keeps coming.

Dwarves

Dwarves have much the same tastes as hobbits and agree with hobbits that meals are best when they are large and frequent. However, dwarves, much more than hobbits, are prepared to subsist on shortened rations for a long time. They take great pride in their ability to endure long, hard marches with little food or drink. Because of their keen ability to handle fire, dwarves are skilled at cooking (another trait they share with hobbits).

Camping Out With Dwarves

Particularly because of their skill in kindling and maintaining fires (even in the worst conditions) and their tendency to make long journeys on tight rations, dwarves are skilled at outdoor cookery. Give them a few rabbits, hares, and possibly a small sheep, and they can make a meal fit for a king—or even a hungry hobbit. Hobbits are good at cooking, too, but only if the meat has been prepared by the butcher and the vegetables have been picked and washed. Dwarves, however, enjoy the down-and-dirty aspects of cooking, from gutting and skinning an animal to plucking a fowl and cutting it up for roasting. The chief lesson here is that hobbits may be more food-centric, but dwarves make the best cooks.

Cram

For their long journeys, many of which take them to lands and places where food is scarce, dwarves have developed a kind of travel cracker called *cram*. It lasts practically forever and can be eaten raw, cooked, or dipped in a little wine or water to soften it. Unfortunately, it tastes like compacted sawdust, and even dwarves admit that a steady diet of *cram* can't be reasonably endured for more than a few weeks. (It does, however, keep you regular if you eat it constantly.) However, *cram* contains enough nutrients to keep an adult dwarf on his feet for a long day of marching and fighting.

Dwarf Ale

Dwarves and hobbits seem to have simultaneously developed the art of brewing ale—at any rate, both claim a long pedigree for their practices, so we can assume they were both doing it at about the same time. Dwarf ale tends to be stronger than the varieties hobbits brew (perhaps because the dwarves' greater body mass can absorb the alcohol). Hobbits, however, create a greater variety of drinks. Not all dwarves like ale; Thorin, for example, drinks red wine when visiting Bilbo, although this seems to be a matter of status as well as taste.

When drinking dwarf ale, drink carefully and slowly. A dwarf, when going strong, is fully capable of drinking you under the table in ten minutes flat. Don't worry if your dwarf companion is ordering his fourth pint while you're still working on your first. There's no rush. Savor the ale going down, and there will be less chance of it coming back up.

Elves

Elves, befitting their ethereal nature, are less attached to food and drink than the other races of Middle-earth. Although they have been known to eat meat, their diet is largely vegetarian—one can imagine elf tofu and other meatless dishes making an appearance at Galadriel's table.

Elf Feasts

The feast given by Elrond Halfelven at Rivendell to celebrate the arrival of Frodo and his companions certainly seems substantial enough. Frodo spends a long time concentrating on his plate before he bothers to look up at his surroundings, so we can assume that Elrond has supplied his guests with food to their liking. At the same time, Elrond himself and his companions don't need much in the way of food.

If you have the good fortune to attend an elf feast, rest assured you will receive a plentiful supply of food that's to your taste. But don't be rude and turn your nose up at roasted acorns or sautéed tree sprouts, or some other sylvan fare. You might actually like it.

Eating on the Road

It so happens that Frodo, Pippin, and Sam have an opportunity to sample elven road food when they leave the Shire. Upon encountering Gildor and some of his companions, the hobbits are invited to take part in a feast in the forest late at night. The food includes "bread, surpassing the savour of a fair white loaf to one who is starving; and fruits sweet as wildberries and richer than the tended fruits of gardens." Not bad for a pick-up meal with a few extra guests. As magical beings, elves don't seem to worry about keeping anything fresh. However, if you get food for a journey from the elves, don't expect it to stay good forever. Eat the bread immediately and it will taste almost as good as it did the night before. Leave it for a few days, and you'll find yourself eating ordinary bread, with just a hint of elvish magic.

Lembas, Elvish Waybread

The elves have their own version of dwarvish *cram*: lembas. In appearance it's similar to *cram*. However, it's far tastier and more nutritious, and it stays good pretty well forever. As an added advantage, orcs (and Gollum) don't like its taste or smell, so they're not likely to eat up your supplies if you're captured (although if you're captured by orcs, food is likely to be the least of your problems).

WAYBREAD BLUEBERRY TART

If, by some chance, you happen to come across a large supply of lembas, consider using it as the basis of other cooking. Here's a quick recipe for Waybread Blueberry Tart:

Crust:
2 cups lembas, crumbled
½ cup shortening
Filling:
1½ cup blueberries, rinsed
½ cup brown sugar
¼ pound butter
⅓ cup blueberry jam

Mix the lembas with the shortening until thick. Press into the bottom of a tart pan. Bake over an open fire until firm (30 minutes, moving to avoid scorching) or in a closed oven at 350 degrees for 20 minutes.

Mix blueberries with jam, and fill tart. Sprinkle lightly with brown sugar and dot with butter. Return to fire or oven and bake until done

Guaranteed to keep the biggest man, elf, or dwarf on his feet for two days. Guaranteed to keep a hobbit on his feet and away from the dinner table for three hours.

Men

Humans have varying tastes in food, depending on where they're from. In the south, near Gondor, foods tend to be more heavily spiced than in the north. This difference reflects the trade between Gondor and other lands such as Rhûn and Harad.

Rangers such as Aragorn are skilled hunters, and meat is an important part of their diets. If you fall in with a party of men, expect a lot of venison (or possibly mutton) roasted on a spit. You'll also find dried fruit, nuts, and cheese. If you eat in one of the higher houses in Minas Tirith, you'll be offered wine and white cakes, along with other well-prepared fare.

Wines of Minas Tirith

Wines in the south of Middle-earth are stronger and earthier than the wines of the north. Southerners prefer red to white and spicy to bland. Minas Tirith is well known for its cellars, and the people of the city are wine connoisseurs of some note. If you're in the neighborhood, stop by the White City for a wine tasting. You won't be sorry.

Dining With the Beornings

Beorn, the huge man (possibly part giant) who keeps open the passes of Mirkwood, is a vegetarian, subsisting mostly on clotted cream, bread, and honey. He evidently doesn't object to the eating of flesh, as he gives the dwarves bows before they set out on their trek through the forest. But he himself doesn't eat it. There isn't word on whether this custom has passed to his descendants, but one presumes they keep up his custom of maintaining bee fields, filled with giant bees as big as hobbits.

If you happen to stop by the house of the Beornings to take afternoon tea, don't baffle and offend your host by asking for the pork pies and sausages. Just eat your cream and honey and bread, and enjoy it.

Ents

Ents deserve a special mention because of the remarkable qualities of their drink. Ents don't eat—or at least no one's ever recorded the sighting of such a thing. But they drink a variety of drinks. Some Ent beverages are like wine and can intoxicate the unwary. Others are like a liquid meal, more satisfying and filling than sitting at board for hours with solid food. Ents, it must be presumed, brew the drinks themselves through some semimagical process. On hobbits, at least, these drinks have a considerable effect, making even fully mature hobbits grow between four and six inches in a matter of several weeks.

How to Drink With the Ents

Keeping in mind that Ents are at least twice (and possibly three times) as tall as you, the first rule is to be polite. Nothing angers an Ent more than someone who's rude—except perhaps someone who's careless with an axe. Second, drink slowly. Third, plan to order new clothes and shoes in a larger size.

Meals in the Shire

In Middle-earth, hobbits are the people most concerned with food and drink and the proper times for each. Since food is one of the centerpieces of their culture, they have elaborate rituals concerning it. (Other people have rituals, too—for instance, the people of Gondor, before each meal, face the West for a moment of silence in tribute to Elvenhome.)

First Breakfast

The hobbit day starts with breakfast, usually at about eight o'clock in the morning. A typical hobbit breakfast will include:

- Bacon
- Eggs
- More bacon
- Cereal
- Coffee
- Ham

    • Stewed tomatoes

First breakfast serves to wake up the hobbit and make sure he's ready
to face the long day ahead—a day of possibly laboring in the fields to
grow more food to sustain him in his quest to grow more food.

    After breakfast, there's the washing up; water has to be hauled
from the well and heated, and dishes need to be scrubbed and set to
dry in the rack. This is wearing work, and afterwards the typical hobbit needs some sustenance.

Second Breakfast

Second breakfast, usually taken at 10:30 a.m., can be eaten on the
front lawn on nice days or possibly in the dining room by an open
window. It includes:

    • Kippered herring
    • Sausages
    • Toast and marmalade
    • Tea
    • Tarts
    • Fried slice
    • More tea

After that's been consumed and a pipe or two smoked, it's time to
clean up the second set of breakfast dishes. At this point, it's time for
Morning Tea, or Elevenses.

Elevenses

This is a light snack, intended to keep a hardworking hobbit going for
a bit until lunchtime. It includes:

    • Scones
    • Biscuits
    • Tea

Elevenses shouldn't take very long—from 11 to possibly 11:45 a.m.,
leaving a decent interval between the end of this meal and luncheon,

which should be served at about 12:30. (Note that in Gondor, Elevenses is sometimes referred to as *Nuncheon* and is partaken by Knights of the City who have risen with first light and haven't eaten since the previous evening's meal. Very few hobbits ever become Knights of the City. Only one, in fact, and he complained a lot about the irregularity of meals.)

Luncheon

This is a significant meal, but it's often taken at a nearby pub, since the hobbit is exhausted from his morning efforts of cooking first breakfast, second breakfast, and elevenses. A hobbit lunch consists of:

- Meat pies
- Cucumber salad
- Stewed tomatoes
- Sausages
- Sandwiches
- Hard-boiled eggs
- Ale—lots of ale

This is accompanied by the after-luncheon pipe (see page 17) and a short nap to recover his strength.

Tea

Teatime in the Shire is practically a religion. Bilbo, when he first goes away with the dwarves, is shocked to discover himself in places where people have never even heard of teatime.

No hobbit is ever really happy unless he or she is within calling distance of a tea kettle. (Bilbo, on the first part of his journey, keeps imagining himself back in his hole with the kettle just beginning to sing on the hob.) But tea consists of much more than the beverage alone. We can form a proper idea of it from the tea Bilbo is forced to give the dwarves and Gandalf when they appear on his doorstep at Bag End:

- Tea
- Ale

- Tarts
- Jam
- Cheese
- Eggs
- Cold chicken
- Pickles
- Biscuits
- Seed-cake
- Buttered scones
- Meat pies
- Fruit pies
- Beer
- Wine
- More tea

(Note that Bilbo doesn't have any difficulty in supplying this enormous amount of food to the party; it's just that the suddenness of it surprises him. It empties out his larders—a good thing, considering that he's going to be out of town for the next year.)

Tea lasts from about 4 p.m. until 6 p.m. After that, there's time for cleaning up and then, later, supper.

Supper

After the enormous tea, supper is a light meal. Nothing too strenuous this late at night. It includes:

- Roast pork
- Bread
- Ham
- Mince-pie
- Vegetables
- Cheese
- Wine
- Ale

And so, to bed. This list doesn't include late-night snacks and sudden fits of midnight munchies, to which many hobbits are subject.

Food for the Average Hobbit

If, by chance, you find yourself with a hobbit houseguest, you'll have to change your food purchasing habits. Here is the minimum of what you'll need for a hobbit for a seven-day week:

- Bread (four loaves)
- Jam (two jars)
- Honey (one jar)
- Eggs (three dozen)
- Pies—meat (five)
- Pies—fruit (three)
- Bacon (five rashers)
- Cheese (two large wheels)
- Assorted fruits
- Chicken (two)
- Beef roast (one, large)
- Pickles
- Beer (one and a half barrels)
- Wine (half a cask)
- Coffee (three gallons)

If the hobbit is young, say, still in his or her tweens—increase these amounts by half.

Pipeweed

Pipeweed is the one pleasure that hobbits claim exclusively for themselves. Indeed, although Gandalf, Aragorn, and Gimli all smoke, they all seem to agree that pipeweed is grown exclusively in the Shire; even Saruman, when he wants to smoke, has to send away for Longbottom Leaf, rather than try to grow his own.

It so happens we know quite a bit about pipeweed, since Meriadoc Brandybuck wrote a short essay on the subject in the introduction to *Herblore of the Shire*.

True Pipeweed

The first true pipeweed of the Shire was grown by Tobold Hornblower
in 1070 (Shire Reckoning), about 350 years before the War of the
Ring. So hobbits had had a considerable amount of time to practice
smoking. Tobold almost certainly got the plant from a hillside near
Bree, so pipeweed had its actual origin outside the Shire. However,
it's the hobbits of the Fourth Farthings who perfected it and cultivated it to its current state.

Meriadoc notes that pipeweed actually grows in the south, around
Gondor, but the people of Minas Tirith don't know what to do with it
and "esteem it only for the fragrance of its flowers." (The people of
Minas Tirith are generally ignorant of the powers of various herbs, as
witnessed by their ignorance regarding the medicinal properties of
kingsfoil in the aftermath of the Battle of the Pelinnor Fields.)

Varieties of Leaf

The only pipeweed we know much about is Longbottom Leaf, made
by the Hornblower family. However, as with beer, each district in
the Shire has its own favored pipeweed that it swears by. Meriadoc
and Pippin smoke Longbottom Leaf because that's what they find
in the ruins of Isengard (part of Saruman's personal stock, despite
his sneers at Gandalf for letting the weed of the halflings cloud his
judgment.) One thing we can be reasonably sure of is that pipeweed,
belonging as it does to the genus *nicotiana*, is addictive. Certainly
Gimli becomes much less grumpy when Merry and Pippin provide
him with some leaf and a pipe to go along with it.

Preparing Pipeweed

Pipeweed, after harvesting, should be dried by laying the leaves out
in the sun. These are then crumbled and stored in leather pouches

for smoking. The quality of pipeweed can be discerned by touch as well as smell. Connoisseurs are even able to make a reasonable guess from touch and smell as to the year of the harvest.

Pipes

The best pipes are baked clay or wood. Wooden pipes, after carving, must be tempered and cured. In general, the longer you smoke a pipe, the better the flavor it will produce, as the layers of pipe smoke are infused into the wood or clay. Clay pipes are considered best by some, but they're easily broken. If you plan to do a lot of traveling that consists of crawling around dark tunnels or climbing fir trees to escape goblins and wolves, a wooden pipe is probably a better choice.

Smoke Rings

Hobbits and wizards (or, at least, one wizard) love to blow smoke rings. In fact, Meriadoc refers to smoking as an "art," and one imagines that Gandalf would agree. The wizard not only blows magical smoke rings in Bilbo's house during the Unexpected Party, he spends valuable time in Beorn's hall blowing smoke rings and sending them chasing one another, dodging around pillars and so on, while Bilbo and the dwarves are stamping with impatience for some news about the intentions of their host. Bilbo has some skill at smoke rings, though there's no sign he passed this ability on to his nephew.

If you want to impress a wizard, try blowing a few smoke rings. At the very least, it'll distract him long enough for you to think up a better strategy.

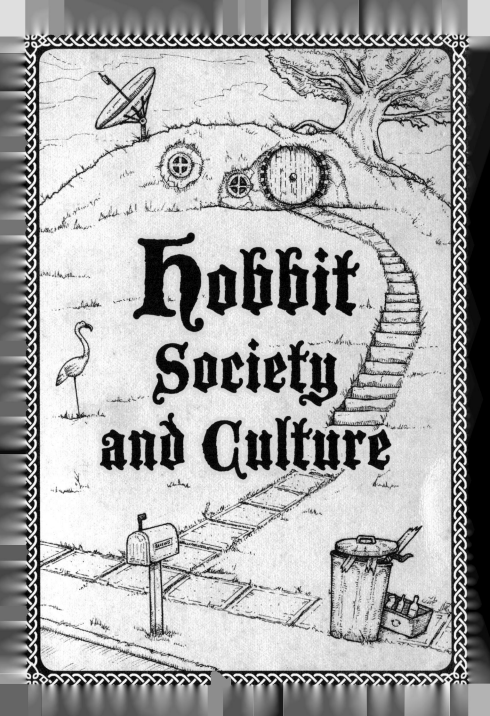

n a hole in the ground there lived a hobbit. Not a nasty, dirty, wet hole, filled with the ends of worms and an oozy smell, nor yet a dry, bare, sandy hole with nothing in it to sit down on or to eat: it was a hobbit-hole, and that means comfort.

—From JRR Tolkien's *The Hobbit*

For hobbits, life in the Shire is a good life. To work hard, play hard, dine regularly, and enjoy the company of neighbors; these are values that are held in high esteem in hobbit culture. At the center of the hobbit way of life is a strict code of etiquette that should be followed at all times. A hobbit should be respectable, polite, and courteous, generous and helpful, and should shy away from trouble, in as such, but in a way that is respectable, polite, courteous, generous, and helpful.

In today's world, humans are too busy to be considerate of each other. They rush around, occupied with everything but accomplishing little. They make little time for family and friends, ignore their neighbors, and eat meals quickly (sometimes without even bothering to sit down). This sort of behavior can only serve to make one more and more ill at ease, impatient, and unhappy.

Hobbits, on the other hand, base their lives on all of the important aspects of community and fellowship. The secret to their happiness lies in their day-to-day focus on relationships with one another and their morals and ethics. It shows in the way they manage their homes, tend their gardens, tackle a day's work, and conduct themselves.

We could all stand to learn a few things from hobbits and their way of life—a way of life that puts family, friends, and neighbors first. The hobbit way of life is one of good manners and consideration of one's fellow man ... or halfling.

Dwellings

One should keep one's home tidy and well managed. After all, you never know when someone may stop by for a visit. A well-stocked larder and wine cellar are of the utmost importance for any hobbit of station.

Even when Bilbo Baggins found himself, to his great surprise, entertaining thirteen dwarves because the wizard Gandalf decided to coerce him into joining their expedition, Bilbo was prepared (for the impromptu dinner party, if not for the adventure itself). Bilbo's neat little hobbit hole was stocked with plenty of seed-cakes, mince-pies, cold chicken, pickles, apple tarts, and beer. In fact, he entertained the dwarves so well that they thought he'd be much more suited as a grocer than a member of their expedition. Bilbo was able to fulfill even the most random refreshment request from the dwarves, so well stocked was his pantry.

Food is obviously important, but one should also always be prepared to make guests feel at home in other ways. You should keep your home tidy and comfortable, and have a plan for guests who may want or need to stay overnight.

A clean and comfortable home, as well as the ability to entertain guests, is a sign of good character. It shows thoughtfulness and consideration. Being a well-prepared host is a duty that everyone should take seriously—hobbits and humans alike.

Comfort and Cleanliness

The home is a reflection of one's character—in fact of one's family's character. It is advisable to keep it neat both inside and out. Your neighbors see your home every day in their comings and goings. If

you don't take care to keep your home in good repair and your garden well managed, neighbors may begin to doubt your good character. And just imagine the first impression such untidiness might make
on a stranger. They might think you're an unruly sort and wrangle you
into a nefarious adventure right then and there. Best to keep things
tidy and avoid trouble.

The inside of your home requires attention as well. You never
know when someone might stop by for a visit. The inside of a hobbit
hole is usually clean, tidy, and practical. Plenty of good space exists
for storing food, and there are lots of pegs for hanging cloaks and
hoods. Any guest would feel most welcome, if a little cozy (hobbits
are small, after all).

When considering your own home, comfort is key. Your abode
should be warm and inviting. There's no need to be extravagant—just
aspire to keep your surroundings neat and comfortable. Try a few
throws and plenty of pillows on the couches and chairs. You'll be living it up hobbit style in no time.

Seating and Accommodations

It's a good idea to have plenty of seating and extra beds (or couches
that can double as beds). Offering a seat is the first kindness a host
should be prepared to extend. And one never knows when one might
need to entertain guests overnight or for an extended time. You may
want to investigate such options as hideaway beds, futons, or built-in
seating along windows—there are plenty of ingenious ideas for maxi-
mizing space that would allow you to accommodate even a troupe of
treasure-hunting dwarves, though why you would want to do that, one
cannot imagine.

The Den

Your den should be cozy with plenty of seating, as you will likely do
most of your entertaining here. For hobbits, the focal point of the
den is usually the hearth. Hobbits might entertain guests by singing a
song or reading a poem by the fireplace.

In today's world, too often the main living room is also the room where humans keep a television. Guests are often plopped down in front of the tube, and before you know it, everyone is sucked in and no one is talking. Is that really quality time with your guests? Instead, consider entertaining like a hobbit might and engaging your guests in conversation and games. Designate a room without a television (or where the television is hidden in a cabinet) for entertaining guests. You'll find the time you spend with your guests much more enjoyable and memorable.

The Study or Library

Hobbits love to read, write, and spend quiet time in their studies. A study or library where one keeps shelves of books, a desk, and important documents is a valuable room to have. A comfortable study is a wonderful place for private conversations or for conducting business. It can also serve as a nice change of location if you want to add some variety to a party. You might have your guests retire to the study for a glass of brandy after dinner.

Sleeping Chambers

Bedrooms should be kept neat, clean, and organized. Always keep the beds made and refresh the linens on a regular basis whether you have company or not (it keeps the beds fresh, for one thing). Other nice touches include keeping a current magazine or an intriguing book on the nightstand. Hobbits always think of the little things, and so should you.

The Bath

Hobbits pride themselves on cleanliness, both of home and of person. One's bathroom should always be kept clean and presentable. Change towels frequently and always make sure you have extra ones for guests. Taking the initiative to quickly tidy your bathroom each day and do a quick spot cleaning will make a world of difference.

You'll not only be ready for unexpected visitors, you'll improve your own quality of life.

The Kitchen

For a hobbit, the kitchen is the most important room in the house. (Actually, that's probably true for anyone, human and halfling alike. Just ask yourself where your guests gravitate whenever you have a party. Odds are they end up standing around in the kitchen with a frothy beverage in hand.)

A hobbit's kitchen is small and neatly organized, but packed full of useful items: pots, pans, spoons, bowls, plates, cups, and saucers. Everything is within quick reach, but somehow kept neatly. Some may call it organized clutter, but a hobbit kitchen is a place where one can easily find whatever is needed. Hobbits usually have a cellar for storing wine, beer, and other items that keep, but most of their ingredients—flour, grains, butter, eggs, fresh vegetables—are kept in a nearby larder. They keep a close watch on their food and rotate their perishables constantly. Nothing has a chance to go bad in a hobbit's kitchen.

Versatility and coziness makes a hobbit kitchen a warm and inviting room where guests enjoy spending time. Guests often pitch in with the cooking and everyone enjoys the food preparation nearly as much as the eating. If you follow the hobbit kitchen example, entertaining your guests might be as easy as handing them a cold beer and inviting them to help you start dinner.

The Garden

While you may think that the inside of your home is what counts, it's a good idea to keep your flower beds and lawn manicured, lest the community begin to think ill of you. Having a well-tended garden will help give the outside of your home an inviting appearance. Your neighbors will be impressed and think highly of you, and any guests you entertain will develop a favorable impression before you even invite them inside (which you should do immediately, by the way).

And besides, gardening is a joy—who doesn't love nature? Nature is a wonderful thing, as long as you have a comfortable home to go back to and you're not off somewhere on an awful adventure, sleeping outdoors. Having a well-kept garden and raising some vegetables is a worthwhile undertaking. Being outside, tending the earth, and watching things grow helps to cultivate calmness and peace of mind. In fact, Samwise Gamgee, who accompanied Frodo Baggins on his quest to throw the Ring of Power into the fires of Mount Doom, was a gardener. The meditative nature of gardening likely contributed to Sam's optimism and patience, which helped him support Frodo on such a dreadful undertaking.

On Entertaining Guests

One should count oneself lucky to have visitors! A visit from someone for a spot of tea or a quick morsel of seed-cake can be the bright spot of any day. Guests should always be held in the highest regard and treated with the proper decorum. A hobbit takes his duty to the well-being of his guests very seriously. One should make a guest feel welcome, with hearty greetings and plentiful refreshments.

In our own lives, we far too often take the easy path and eat out at a local restaurant or tavern. We avoid entertaining in the home, opting instead for a quick happy hour at the local pub (actually, that sounds like a valid choice when thinking like a hobbit). But having visitors can be a great pleasure, despite the work involved. Consider storing a few extra bottles of wine, stocking some beer or soda, and keeping some snacks on hand, and soon you'll be entertaining in grand hobbit style. Remember to always keep your ice trays full, and form the habit of offering a little something whenever someone stops by. Your friends will think you very resourceful and will appreciate your generous hospitality.

Welcoming Guests

Never keep a guest waiting on the doorstep. Make sure to invite them in quickly and offer to take their coats, hats, cloaks, hoods, or outer garments of choice. Offer them a place to sit straightaway—a guest's comfort should be your utmost concern.

Next, offer refreshments. If it is a quick visit, tea and cakes are usually appropriate. If the visit is a lengthy one or if it is close to a mealtime, invite the guest to join you for the meal.

In the case that the visit isn't a social one, but instead a matter of business, you may wait until after matters have been discussed to offer refreshment.

The Host's Duty

Hobbits are highly concerned with making their guests feel wanted. Even when Bilbo found his home filled with dwarves who were seeking adventure, of all things, he did his best to entertain them.

As a host, one should always offer guests the first choice of all refreshments. In the unfortunate instance that there isn't enough for everyone, the host should politely do without, making excuses of having had a rather large second breakfast. This may be a difficult sacrifice; however, be careful not to show disappointment. Look to your duties and be gracious.

Overnight Guests

When one has overnight guests, make every attempt to provide proper accommodations. If possible, guests should have a room of their own, even if the host has to give up his own room and sleep on the couch.

Be sure to provide fresh bed linens, towels, washcloths, and a bottle of water or designated tumbler for drinking water.

Passersby

One should greet folks passing by with a hearty "Good Morning" (or "Good Afternoon" or "Good Evening," depending on the time of day).

Small talk about the weather is recommended, especially if it is a fine day. Offer the person a spot of tea or a pipe of whatever leaf you're smoking. Nothing can complement a fine day more than sharing in life's little pleasures.

Greeting strangers is more than just a kindness; you never know who a stranger may turn out to be. The day Bilbo met Gandalf, he was simply enjoying a nice morning when the wizard happened by. Bilbo greeted him kindly, though he suspected Gandalf capable of mischief, which he was, of course. But in the end they became the best of friends.

Unexpected Guests

When an unexpected guest drops by for a visit, one should do one's best to make them feel welcome and comfortable. Invite them to sit and offer them whatever refreshments you have on hand.

Unwelcome Guests

In the case of an unwelcome guest, it is still important to uphold your duty as host. Though you are in a difficult position, you should remain pleasant and cordial. It is still advisable to make time for a polite conversation and offer refreshment. Anything less would be rude.

When Guests Overstay Their Welcome

Hobbits have an interesting approach to dealing with guests who stay longer than what is considered a reasonable time (for hobbits this is more than a month; as a human, it's considerably less). Hobbits rarely ask someone to leave. Instead, when a guest shows no signs of leaving, a hobbit will inform them that they are now a member of the household and begin to assign them household duties.

You may want to employ this tactic with guests who stay too long. You'll likely find that it works like a charm, and they'll be looking for somewhere else to go rather quickly.

When Approached by a Solicitor

Even when dealing with solicitors you should employ a measure of politeness and decorum. Thank them for extending their gracious offer, even if it is something as deplorable as being involved in an adventure. After thanking them, you may decline their kind offer and wish them "Good Day."

Being a Guest

Hobbits are generally careful to be good guests. They are considerate of their host and try to employ all of their good manners lest they damage their reputation. To impose upon one's host is a terrible social blunder.

From time to time one may have the occasion to be a guest either in someone's home or in a setting such as a gathering, party, or outing. It is of the utmost importance to conduct oneself in such a manner as to be the sort of guest that a host is glad to see and welcomes with open arms.

Invitations and RSVPs

Upon receiving an invitation to a gathering or special occasion, one should make every attempt to respond as soon as possible. It is rude to keep your host guessing how many will attend her affair. It should go without saying that one should always remember to thank the host for extending the invitation, whether you accept or decline.

Arriving on Time

One should make every attempt to arrive at an occasion near the appointed time. To arrive early may interrupt your host's attempts to make final preparations and may cause them undue stress. Arriving late in order to make a grand entrance shows a disregard for your host's position as the center of attention and is, quite simply, rude.

Gift for the Host

Hobbits always try to bring along a small token of thanks for their host, be it a bottle of wine or a freshly baked loaf of bread. Human or halfling, it's always a good idea to bring a little something along to show your appreciation for being invited.

Staying Overnight

On the occasion that one stays overnight, one should respect the host's personal routine and make every effort to adhere to their schedule, retiring for the evening and rising in the morning at their usual time. You may be unaccustomed to keeping their hours, but make an attempt so you don't disrupt your host's day-to-day life. You are a guest, after all.

Extended Stays

In the event that one is staying with a host for a longer period of time, one should offer to help with any household chores: cleaning, tidying, or preparing meals. One should be careful not to overstay one's welcome. Watch for signs that your welcome may be wearing thin. It's better to leave early and express regrets if you notice your host is tiring of your company, though, any good host will undoubtedly make every attempt to hide it.

Social Behavior

Society is very important to hobbits. They love feeling like they are part of a community and spend much of their time visiting friends and neighbors, participating in Shire events, and socializing. Naturally, they dedicate a great deal of thought and energy to practicing proper etiquette.

Hobbits take behavior and decorum very seriously. The way one conducts oneself in public or in the company of others is crucial to maintaining one's reputation. Being humble, gracious, and courteous are signs of good character.

Keeping Appointments

Hobbits take keeping appointments quite seriously. However, they are busy little folks and are prone to forgetfulness from time to time—there are so many people to visit and so many meals to prepare and enjoy, after all. Bilbo was fond of keeping an engagement tablet so that he wouldn't forget his appointments. It's a good idea to do the same. A handy pocket calendar will do the trick (or, being a human in the days of men, you may want to simply enter reminders on your smartphone). Just make sure you don't miss a single commitment!

Correspondence

Hobbits have an affinity for writing letters. They can be very long-winded, using florid language that often verges on poetry (they enjoy poetry very much). In today's world people often don't take enough time to really correspond with others. They send quick e-mails, texts, or tweets. But how can you convey true emotion and sentiment using such limited mediums? Take some time once in a while to handwrite a thoughtful card or letter. It will convey more than just words and is sure to be appreciated.

Making Speeches

Hobbits can be long-winded. Their speeches will likely go on and on (and on) with lots of references to lineage and nods to tradition. This is probably one area of hobbit culture that you might consider an unnecessary pursuit, unless you simply love to hear yourself talk. In fact, just forget we ever mentioned it.

Listening to Speeches

Hobbits are very gracious listeners. When other people are speaking, they pay attention, seemingly hanging on every word (aside from elder hobbits, who often fall asleep but are excused because of their age and station in the Shire). When someone is speaking you should do your very best to be attentive—even if the person is a tiresome orator. Save your own comments, questions, or anecdotes for after they've finished; you'd expect to be afforded the same consideration.

Accepting Honors or Awards

When receiving an award or some form of recognition, hobbits consider it polite to make mention of thanks to each hobbit lineage by family name, from Bagginses to Zaragambas. One should be careful when planning an acceptance speech, so as not to show favor to one friend or family member over another. Being gracious when you accept an honor is a way to show good character, so make sure you give credit to everyone—even to those you don't feel deserve it. Speeches are not times to make pointed remarks or to get in a dig at someone. Always take the higher path.

Paying the Check

When it comes to picking up the check, you can learn a lot from hobbits, who typically make a grand display of manners when it comes time to settle up at a tavern or restaurant. Everyone will offer to pay for everyone else. They can go on for hours saying things like, "No, no … it's my turn," or "Oh, but I believe you paid last time," or "But you stopped by the other day with those lovely seed-cakes," and so on. It's important to actually remember whose turn it is. That person should pick up the tab or risk damage to his reputation. When you truly can't remember whose turn it is, a good solution may be to order another round and preemptively pay for that round while the rest of the party works out the mystery amongst themselves. You'll have paid your share, and your companions will be grateful for the aid you've provided in sorting out the dilemma—after an extra pint, everything should make perfect sense.

Giving Gifts

In the age of man, gift giving has gotten out of control. Holiday spending has become an obligatory source of stress. Many people often give gifts with the intention of one-upping each other or because they don't want to receive a gift without having given one. In their minds, everyone must be even steven, fair and square. They don't even realize they're going to all this trouble for the wrong reasons. And with the senseless rush to buy presents for everyone and the temptation to exceed the value of gifts given the year before, the whole thing has escalated to a madness somewhat akin to the Battle of Helms Deep. Just ask anyone who's ever been in a 3-mile radius of a shopping mall during the holidays. One might prefer to face a horde of rampaging orcs.

Hobbits, on the other hand, have a more laid-back approach to gift giving. Gifts are given, but they are usually simple and thoughtful: homemade baked goods, small toys for children, or a useful item crafted by hand (a small piece of furniture, perhaps). Most important, gifts are never expected, nor are they given out of obligation.

Delivering Good News

Hobbits love to deliver good news. Good news is usually conveyed alongside delicious food, tankards of ale, and plenty of pipeweed to go around. In order to deliver the news properly, hobbits figure that it is best to sample the ale and have a pipe or two before guests arrive, in order to achieve the proper mood and also to make sure the offerings are worthy of the occasion. Humans usually wait for everyone to arrive at their gathering before enjoying such refreshments. But why endure waiting on such a celebratory occasion? Best to make the most of it and enjoy the mood. Just make sure you have plenty of fine refreshments; your friends will be so delighted with your good news that they won't mind that you've already tucked in, and will likely have no problem quickly catching up. The celebrations will be in full swing in no time.

Delivering Bad News

Bad news is never fun to deliver. Hobbits usually try to soften the blow by making sure there is ample comfort food, many tankards of ale, and plenty of pipeweed to go around. In order to deliver the news properly, hobbits figure that it is best to sample the ale and have a pipe or two in order to brace themselves and also to make sure the offerings might help lift dampened spirits. Humans usually wait for everyone to arrive before taking sustenance, but when dealing with bad news one may need a little something just to get through the day. Best to take the edge off so you may lend a strong shoulder to others. Just make sure you have plenty of supplies on hand; your friends won't begrudge you sustenance under the circumstances, and given the seriousness of the situation they'll likely have no problem catching up. The commiseration will be well underway in no time.

Relationships and Family

Little is more important to a hobbit than family and friends. They sing songs about the kindness and character of their ancestors. Their whole lifestyle is planned around fellowship in the community. Hobbits always think of others first and foremost.

Friendship

It has already been mentioned that hobbits are fiercely loyal friends. The bond of friendship is nearly as important to a hobbit as bonds with their own family. Hobbits will do almost anything for a friend, as evidenced by the way Sam, Merry, and Pippin quickly join Frodo on his ring quest in spite of the many dangers they know they will face. The hobbits had several chances to turn back or avoid battle, but each one rose to the occasion to stand alongside his friends. Anyone who can say they have a friend as loyal as a hobbit is truly blessed.

Courtship

Hobbits tend to marry after a courtship of at least several months—sometimes years—during which the couple engages in such respectable activities as dancing and going for walks. Hobbits exchange courting gifts, usually flowers from the male and baked goods from the female. On occasion, humans rush into marriage. The hobbits' courtship customs are a good reminder that it's important to allow for a lengthy engagement so that love and friendship for one's betrothed may blossom and grow.

Marriage

Hobbit marriages typically occur outdoors in the spring and the entire Shire usually attends. Much like human ceremonies, the bride wears a dress (often white), while the bridegroom wears a good shirt and his very best vest. They exchange poetic vows and then have a great outdoor feast accompanied by beer, wine, singing, and dancing.

In many ways, hobbit weddings are very much like human weddings. One notable exception is the absence of line dancing. If humans could learn one thing from hobbits, and one thing only, it might be that they should never have invented the Electric Slide.

Raising Children

Hobbits, with their love of family and community, are naturally wonderful parents. They are incredibly nurturing and protective of their young. Young hobbits, known as faunts, are often playful and may show an interest in mischief and adventure. This behavior is tolerated to a certain age, as hobbits hope that allowing such follies in youth will allow children to get it out of their systems early instead of going off on some foolish quest later in life. As humans often say, but just as often forget, "Kids will be kids." Be sure to teach your kids good values, but remember that children need to play and have their fun so they can be upstanding adults when the time comes.

Siblings

In hobbit culture, siblings are usually very close. They've played together, worked the fields together, and grown up together. If hobbit friends are close, then siblings are usually even closer—often becoming business partners as they assume the family vocation. Unlike human society, you don't see much sibling rivalry among hobbits—

they know there is plenty of love and mutual respect to go around, as long as everyone carries their fair share of the load.

Parents

Hobbits treat their parents with the utmost respect. Young hobbits, for the most part, strive to make their parents proud. They typically work hard at learning the family trade and most assume their parents' line of work. Later in life, as their parents age, hobbits do whatever is needed to care for their parents and to keep them comfortable and happy (hobbits tend to lead quite long lives, so the bond between parents and children is a very strong one). While humans today may live much farther away and often pursue professions outside the family trade, it is still important to keep close ties with your parents. Don't get so caught up in your own routine that you forget to show your parents love and appreciation. We owe our parents our lives, quite literally.

Extended Family

Uncles, aunts, and cousins are always welcome. An unspoken standing invitation prevails among hobbit family members, and one's home is always open to family (even distant relatives). Hobbits tend to keep close contact with members of their extended families, often designating a day of the week for an extended family gathering. They also write plenty of letters and share all of the latest news and gossip. As humans, we really have no excuse not to follow the hobbit example and keep closer contact with our families—in this day and age of the Internet and social media.

Elders

Elder hobbits have an important place in hobbit society. They are revered for their wise council and often serve as leaders in the community. Younger hobbits are eager to lend their elders a hand with chores, and they stop in to check on them frequently, often bringing them a loaf of freshly baked bread, a pie, or a pouch of

Longbottom Leaf. Always remember, your elders have the wisdom of experience, and if you are kind to them, they'll likely reward you with valuable advice.

Work

Hobbits believe in good, honest work. Favored hobbit occupations include farming, gardening, carpentry, masonry, and butchering. Hobbits love to make things with their hands and believe that items should be well prepared or well crafted, otherwise one might as well not bother. A day's work is something one should take pride in. One should do one's best and commit fully to the task at hand. In your own work, no matter what it is, the hobbit's approach will serve you well. That said, hobbits also believe in taking full advantage of leisure time. One should always pause in work for the purpose of regular meals, naps, and leisurely activities.

Leisure

When it comes to pleasures in life, leisure comes in second only to food for hobbits. Halflings are fond of music and poetry; they enjoy singing and making up funny songs to entertain each other. They use any chance they can for celebration and love any occasion to dance. Hobbits enjoy sport and will engage in such lawn games as quoits, bowls, or ninepins. In taverns they enjoy a good game of darts.

Music

Hobbits enjoy music of all kinds. Most of their songs are lighthearted ditties, drinking songs, and ballads or folk songs that recount tales passed down from their ancestors. Most hobbits won't admit it, but they also enjoy hearing songs of foreign lands, adventure, and heroes. While they shy away from adventure, they love a good tale, especially in the form of an epic ballad. The lesson hobbits give humans on music is to listen with a nonjudgmental ear and to appreciate the songs of other cultures. You'll enjoy music all the more if you do.

Dancing

Dancing comes naturally to hobbits. Any creature that goes barefoot all the time is bound to love doing a soft shoe once in a while. Hobbit dancing is typically very jolly, with lots of bouncing around and kicking of one's feet. Hobbits dance more for fun than for expression. You won't find a lot of artistic interpretation going on in a hobbit dance— no dark or suggestive undertones. No bumping or grinding or popping and locking. Just good clean fun. Now, doesn't that sound nice?

Reading

Books are a joy to hobbits, who love to read all kinds of stories and poems, from tales of the old days to stories of the elves, many of which are full of adventure and treasure (a guilty pleasure for hobbits). Hobbits love to share books with one another, and they keep detailed records of the contents of their libraries, who they lent books to, and notes on what the reader said about the book upon returning it. For hobbits, books are more than just stories; they are treasured items to be handled, dog-eared, shared, and passed down as heirlooms.

Today we rarely appreciate the thought and care put into the narrative. We don't savor books and take time to consider all the experiences writers must have drawn upon when writing them. Books have become disposable and impermanent. Want to get the most out of life the way a hobbit would? Want to experience that authentic feeling of holding something old and treasured in your hands—sort of like a ring of power, only without the side effects of a pesky evil influence? Try picking up a real book once in a while.

Writing

Hobbits are very thoughtful creatures and enjoy keeping detailed chronicles of their daily lives. They are quick to take up the pen and

spend the day recording their thoughts, visits with other folks, and tales of their ancestors, often embellishing details. In the event that they find themselves involved in some adventure, hobbits will fill volumes and volumes with the details of everything they saw, smelled, ate, and experienced. Even a dreadful situation makes a good story, and hobbits love a good story almost as much as they love food.

Sport

If you visit the Shire on any given day, you'll see hobbits engaged in any number of games—outdoor games with balls or discs, games of chess or checkers, tavern games, and the like. Hobbits love to play. The rules of the games are sometimes hard to discern, as they can be changed on a whim. Hobbits aren't usually very competitive, and the game itself isn't as important to them as the act of playing. Spending time with friends at any diversion is what they enjoy.

Humans can be so obsessed with rules that the games they play can cease to be fun and occasionally lead to fights. Even spectator sports, which may start with a simple rivalry between fans of different teams, can from time to time erupt into all-out brawls. Best to follow the example of hobbits and remember that it's only a game, after all.

Smoke Rings

Smoking may be the hobbit's favorite pastime. The hobbits invented the art of smoking pipeweed, an herb cultivated in the Shire after it was introduced to the region by Númenóreans, who were men from a distant land. The Rangers of the North and the dwarves call it Halflings's Leaf. It's an herb of numerous varieties: Longbottom Leaf, Southern Star, Old Toby. Each is named after the area of the Shire it is grown in.

Hobbits smoke the herb using pipes made of clay or wood. The burning leaves produce a rich, thick smoke that is excellent for blowing smoke rings. Hobbits can spend entire afternoons blowing rings of different sizes, shapes, and configurations and watching them soar into the sky. Much like cloud gazing, they'll watch the shapes drift and change, and they'll think of different things those shapes might look like.

It's all a complete waste of time, of course. And an unhealthy habit to boot. But who are humans to judge with all the different— and often much worse—drugs and chemicals some of them imbibe? And heck, doesn't everyone deserve to spend a lazy day looking up at the sky once in a while? (For more discourse on pipeweed, see "Concerning Food, Drink, and Pipeweed" on page 3).

On Parties

Occasions worth celebrating should not be taken lightly. Hobbit parties consist of plenty of food, beer, and dancing. And while consorting with wizards is normally considered deplorable, turning a blind eye for parties is recommended since wizards tend to share wonderful stories and fireworks.

As humans, we all know someone who is full of mischief and can cause trouble the same way a wizard can. If you want to make your party an occasion to remember, you might consider inviting that person. It may not be a good idea, but it will certainly make for a memorable party.

Holidays

Hobbits love holidays. A couple of prominent holidays in hobbit culture are Lithe, which is a midsummer holiday celebrated with feasting and merriment, and Yule, which is a midwinter holiday celebrated with feasting and merriment. Celebrations for both holidays can last weeks or months, so you can imagine the sheer amount of feasting and merriment to be had. Simple gifts may be given as part of hobbit holiday celebrations but are given freely and never out of obligation. People can look to hobbits as a reminder of what holidays should really be about, and that is fellowship.

Wealth

Hobbits are typically quite good with managing wealth. Bilbo had plenty of money that he'd inherited from his ancestors, particularly from the Took side of his family (the Tooks were rather adventurous for hobbits and had accumulated quite a bit of wealth). Bilbo never lived extravagantly—hobbits rarely do—but instead used his wealth to live comfortably and to extend kindnesses to others, including his unexpected dwarf houseguests at the beginning of his adventures.

Humans would do well to follow the example of hobbits in handling their own money. Managing your finances in a smart way is undoubtedly a good practice, but money can easily corrupt you and make you greedy. Remember to share your good fortune, and you'll not only make someone else's day but you'll be doing yourself a service as well.

Greed

In the final chapters of *The Hobbit*, Bilbo and the dwarves find themselves under siege by men of Esgaroth, asking for a percentage of the dragon Smaug's treasure to use for rebuilding their town after it was destroyed by Smaug. Thorin, leader of the dwarves, feels that the men had no claim to the treasure, as it originally belonged to Thorin's ancestors. Bilbo, realizing that the two forces are at the brink of war, uses his portion of the treasure to negotiate an amiable resolution. Ultimately, he offers his share of the treasure to the men to rebuild their town.

Bilbo's example reminds us that money should be used for the greater good. Bilbo saw the plight of the men who were threatening his friends and was able to empathize when the dwarves could not. Bilbo knew that his portion of the treasure—no matter how great it was—was less important than helping people in need and finding a peaceful resolution to the conflict.

Repaying Debts

On his return journey, Bilbo gifts the Wood-elf king a necklace in thanks for providing bread and wine. In this way Bilbo demonstrates the importance of repaying your debts. In doing so you will maintain friendships and alliances that may be useful to you again some other day. Plus, it's simply the right thing to do.

Taking Only What You Need

Before returning to the Shire, Bilbo and Gandalf stop off to reclaim some treasure they buried after a narrow escape from trolls. Bilbo took a couple saddlebags of gold and silver and offered the rest to Gandalf. Bilbo simply felt he had all he needed. Hobbits are rarely greedy. They know what they need in order to live comfortably and know that anything more will likely serve to make their lives more complicated. What do you need to live a comfortable life? Seriously consider this question and keep in mind that grasping for anything more often leads to unhappiness.

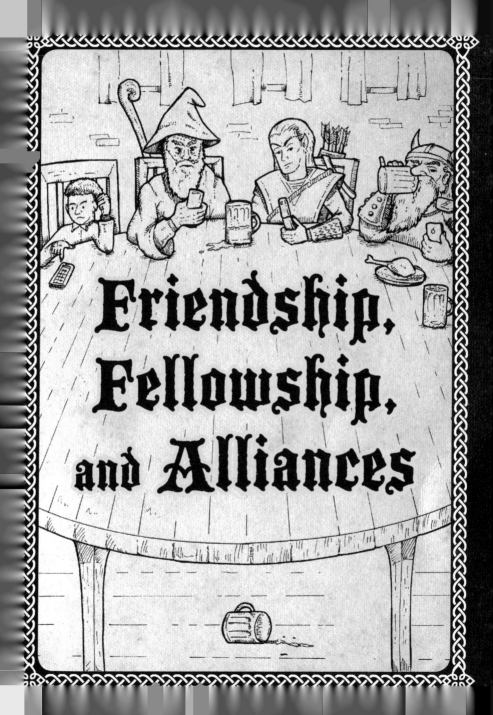

Friendship, Fellowship, and Alliances

You can trust us to stick to you, through thick and thin—to the bitter end. And you can trust us to keep any secret of yours—closer than you keep it yourself. But you cannot trust us to let you face trouble alone, and go off without a word. We are your friends, Frodo."

—Merry in JRR Tolkien's
The Fellowship of the Ring

If you're like most people in Middle-earth, hobbits are not the first free folk who come to mind when you think of alliances or fellowships. They're an unlikely race for adventures, both by stature and preference.

For friendship ... yes, you might consider a hobbit. Especially if you're of the type who loves a good party and wishes to enjoy it with others of like mind.

Let us explore how hobbits fit into the world of friendship, fellowship, and alliances, and what wisdom they may offer us Big Folk.

Friendship

Hobbits are all about a good party. More than any other race in Middle-earth, hobbits can be counted upon to pull a friend into The Green Dragon for a night of drinking, feasting, dancing, and singing. In fact, if it weren't for the womenfolk and the call of a bright garden needing tending, male hobbits would spend their every waking hour in the friendly alliance of fellowship.

It is this playful innocence, this bucolic simplicity, that Strider and his Rangers and so many others—including a number of hobbits—made deep sacrifices to protect.

Life Is Better With a Friend

Hobbits are a communal people. They are not given to striking out on their own or exploring—much less passing—the boundaries of the Shire. Bilbo broke this habit only by what almost amounts to kidnapping, and Frodo evidently inherited some strange wanderlust from his uncle. But all hobbits would rather be homebodies, if given the chance.

What could be better than sitting in your rocking chair on the back porch on a pleasant Hobbiton evening, smoking pipeweed? The only thing better, in a hobbit's mind, would be doing so with a friend.

Perhaps all hobbits are extroverts. Perhaps they become energized by being with one another. One would think there would exist at least a few loners who recover their energy not by being with other hobbits but by being alone. And yet, it seems they all tend to seek company rather than solitude.

A lesson we might take from the hobbits is that there is something to be said for companionship. The evening is sweeter, the meal is more savory, and the moment is simply finer when experienced with a friend.

Hard moments, too, are endured more easily when a companion is there to help bear the load, as Merry points out at the opening of our chapter.

What would hobbits be like in our day of Facebook and Twitter? Each one would probably have as many friends as there are hobbits. Excepting those who live toward Bree, where both the news and the hobbits are often strange. And perhaps excepting those hobbits who go out on boats. But all the rest would be friends.

If humans can spend all day on Facebook, what might hobbits do? They might never emerge from their holes in the ground. And yet they would be utterly delighted to have spent that time engaged with friends, old and new.

And can you imagine Pippin with an iPhone? The poor lad would be torn between laughing with his friends at the pub and LOL-ing with his friends over texts.

Most of us could do with a bit more LOL-ing in our lives, and good friends are the best source of this. Let us take a cue from the hairy-footed hobbits and seek out friends with whom to enjoy the precious days of our lives.

Make Friends Wherever You Go

A difference lies between friendliness and friendship. As we have seen elsewhere in this book, hobbits have hospitality down to a science. But that is a cultural expectation to be extended even to those guests who are not friends at all. True friendship goes beyond being cordial.

Ideally, of course, every hobbit gets to stay home and be sensible, tending to one's affairs and enjoying the Bolgers, Hornblowers, and Proudfoots (Proudfeet!) of one's own village.

But occasionally, either by ill-advised choice or unpleasant turn of events, some unfortunate hobbits are forced to travel—even beyond the borders of the Shire, to the land of the Big Folk. If such a trip must be made, it should be done with one's friends. But every once or twice in an age, a hobbit goes alone on an unexpected journey.

In such cases, what is a hobbit to do but continue his habits until such time as he can stop being there and go back again? He must continue to offer kindnesses to visitors. He must continue to offer counsel about well-ordered gardens and good tilled earth. And, of course, he must maintain his practices of enjoying food, drink, pipe-weed, song, and the finest thing in life: friendship.

When a hobbit finds himself in an unfamiliar place, surrounded by unfamiliar companions of good character, he must do his best to befriend them. If you can't stay at the party you were enjoying, and if you can't bring the party with you, why not make a new party here?

Who knows but that the Bifur and Bofur beside you might become your dearest hearth mates? Acquaintances unlooked-for might actually be best friends previously unmet. If you can't be with the one you love, hobbit, love the one you're with.

In the world of men, we can't always choose our companions. We might venture on a business trip to meet people we've never encountered before, not to mention our seatmates on the plane along the way. It's much more pleasant to stay at home with our comfortable circle of friends. But sometimes the people we meet can become delightful new additions to that circle, which thereby widens just a bit.

A certain man went on a trip to teach at a conference. Very much against his wishes he was given a roommate who was also on faculty at the conference. The double room was a nuisance. Wasn't it enough that he would be out among the people for the duration of the conference? Was it too much to ask to have a private retreat at the hotel?

The roommate didn't arrive until after midnight the first night. Our hero feigned sleep so as to not have to interact. Inevitably the next morning came, and the two exchanged the obligatory information about one another. It happened that the roommate liked one of our hero's favorite movies. And that he felt the same way our hero did about certain topics. And that they liked the same bands, were teaching complementary ideas at the conference, and pulled for similar sports teams. Not least of all, the two found an easy compatibility in each other.

In short, these two were best friends who simply hadn't met yet.

Neither would have met the other—neither would've had his life enriched—had they not left their comfort zones and taken a lesson from hobbits to befriend those they found themselves beside. The next time you're somewhere with others you don't know—the subway or the waiting room at the mechanic's shop or in line at Walmart—don't neglect the opportunity to make a new friend. Begin by complimenting something about the person or his or her belongings or apparel, and off you'll go.

A Hobbit and His Squire

It has been pointed out that the friendship we see between Frodo and Sam is analogous to the British gentleman and his chief man-servant. The knight and his squire. The master and his apprentice. Hobbits ascribe to the time-honored tradition of the younger one learning the older one's wisdom. Among male and female, lord and peasant, there is much to be gained by paying attention to the transmission of knowledge from the teacher to the student. So Frodo learns Elvish from Bilbo, and Samwise learns gardening from his old Gaffer. The womenfolk among the hobbits likewise pass on skills in their realms of expertise.

Every one of us, even outside the Shire, ought to have both a mentor and a disciple. Do you have someone to whom you can go when you seek wisdom? If not, see about developing such a relationship. The learned among us can be found in business organizations, churches, and synagogues, and especially the Internet. Why not offer to take one of them to lunch to see if there might be a compatibility there?

In the same way, you have much to offer those younger or less experienced than you. You could become a mentor. This doesn't mean being boorish and assuming that you are superior to others and that they should flock to you for your pearls of wisdom and ascribe to your obviously superior methods. It means being approachable and free with the secrets of your success. It means believing that you have something to offer that might result in someone else's success and being willing to lavish it on a willing learner. If you don't have a disciple in your circle, perhaps you might develop one in one or more fields in which you have earned a measure of success or expertise.

Frodo and Sam are friends across a sort of social divide. Though there isn't a hobbit aristocracy exactly, there are still those who are better off and those who live (and eat) at the homes of the better off.

Perhaps for them, a better analogy than knight and squire would be officer and sergeant. There are—in the militaries of Gondor, Rohan, and the United States—two separate tracks of rank advancement: that of officers and that of the enlisted. The tracks run parallel but are not considered equal. Traditionally officers have risen from the more highly educated and monied families, whereas enlisted men in the rank and file have come from the wider stock of the nation from which the army is raised.

One might assume that an officer and an enlisted man, or NCO (non-commissioned officer), would be unlikely friends. Surely the divergent duties and powers of the two would make it an uneven friendship at best. But throughout history there are many examples of this sort of friendship.

Sometimes we encounter kindred spirits in unexpected places. It's not always our peers who make the best friends. It might be the person on the other side of the world, whose life situation is radically different from our own, who becomes a soul mate of sorts. The trick is to look for such friends wherever you go.

Frodo and Sam are friends across a social divide, as previously mentioned. Frodo could play the lordly patron and constantly remind Sam of his lowborn status, but he doesn't. He treats Sam as a peer. Neither does Sam consider himself a worthless peon who has nothing of value to offer. He counts himself as worthy and valid.

We all have to remember the station our situation places us in—employer or employee, customer or manager, upperclassman or lowerclassman. However, we shouldn't make more of that station than it is. We must not believe our worth is based on our status.

Perhaps your next dear friend will be your instructor at the gym. Perhaps it will be the shopping cart kid at the grocery store. Perhaps it will be the Russian you've befriended on an online forum about pottery or World War II memorabilia. When we decide not to let our birth differences segregate us, potential friends present themselves to us.

So whether you're from the gentry or the peasantry—or whatever your social status—take a lesson from Frodo and Sam, and look for amicability in all your relationships.

True Friendship

You would be hard-pressed to find, in literature, a better example of true friendship than that which Tolkien produced in *The Lord of the Rings* (LOTR). The friendship among the Fellowship, the friendship between Gimli and Legolas, and the friendship among the four hobbits are excellent illustrations of the lengths friends will go for one another.

But the pinnacle of friendship in LOTR is between Frodo and Sam. When we say we would go to the ends of the earth for someone, we usually don't think we'll have to. But that's exactly what Samwise the Brave did for Frodo. Sam left his gardening, his taters, his Gaffer, and his sense of safety behind and strode off toward an uncertain doom.

If you searched the Shire from top to Longbottom, you'd not find a more sensible hobbit than Sam. He's as hobbit as hobbit gets. He was from fine stock and on a path to being herbmaster before too many more years had passed. Yet, off he went, out of Bag End like one of Gandalf's fireworks.

Speaking of that wizard, Gandalf charged Sam not to leave Frodo's side as they journeyed to Rivendell. But he needed no Grey Wizard to tell him that.

Sam was loyal to Frodo beyond the bonds of mere acquaintanceship or the noble loyalty of a servant to his master. This was the fiercest kind of friendship, one that bears very little difference from love. And before it was over, Sam would stand before monsters, orcs, goblins, Ents, and traitors, and on the lip of the Cracks of Doom, all for his friend.

Frodo's friendship for Sam is equal to Sam's for him. To take the Ring at all was an act of heroism of the first order. And what is heroism but friendship of a dramatic sort? Frodo's friendship for Sam involved protecting him from the burden of the Ring so far as he could. It was true that Frodo wouldn't have gotten far without Sam, but there is no doubt that Sam wouldn't have gotten past Farmer Maggot's field had it not been for Frodo. They helped each other along the way, even when it came to self-sacrifice.

Frodo took up the Ring and vowed to move it away from the Shire in order to protect his people. Of course that meant removing himself from the Shire, as well. Probably a portion of Frodo didn't mind the journey, having a bit of the Took in him. (Tooks longed for adventure.) And Bilbo's tale of going there and back again rang loudly in his ears. Removing the danger from the world of hobbits was a truly generous gesture.

Other hobbits displayed loyalty and heroism that amounts to friendship of a true sort. Fatty Bolger, Merry, Pippin, and Farmer Maggot played their parts well. What no one knew and old Gandalf suspected was that hobbits are not mere children, made soft by how completely they've been protected. They are hardy and resourceful and courageous beyond anyone's estimation. At the heart of the Fellowship that saved Middle-earth was the friendship of hobbits.

Who would you go to the ends of the earth for? Would you leave the comfort and safety of your home if it might mean danger and sacrifice? For whom would you march into Mordor?

And do those people know you would do that for them? Maybe it's time you told them.

Friendship isn't just parties and feasting. Friendship is self-sacrifice for the benefit of those you cherish.

Fellowship

Fellowship is a form of friendship and companionship that has special meaning in the world of Middle-Earth—and in our world as well.

Fellowship as a Noun

A fellowship is a band of companions united toward a common purpose and quest. Bilbo's fellowship was with Gandalf and the dwarves.

Frodo's fellowship was with representatives of all the free races: elves, dwarves, men, wizards, and hobbits. Their mutual goals, and their pursuit of those goals, bound these people into a powerful, albeit temporary, force.

Are you a member of a fellowship? Are you on a team or task force or committee formed to advance something you believe in? Your life will be richer if you join such a group. Shared experiences—hardships, victories, and even defeats—unite people in lasting ways.

A certain couple adopted a child from China. They worked with an American adoption agency that arranged the travel details. When at last it was time to board the plane for Asia, the couple didn't know anyone in their travel group. When they arrived in Beijing, they began meeting the other adoptive families. In all, there were thirteen families traveling together to one province in China to adopt their new family members.

After touring Beijing with one set of local guides, the group boarded a flight to their target province in China's interior, where other guides took them through the process of getting their children. After a week or so with the new babies, the whole group boarded another flight and flew to a third province, where a third set of guides helped them through the sequence of finalizing the adoption.

Through it all, that core group of families grew closer as a fellowship. The local guides were wonderful but didn't become members of the group. Only the adoptive families—and then the babies—remained as they traveled from place to place. The families helped each other, went to Chinese groceries for each other, borrowed and lent and compared with each other, ate and drank together. In short, they grew a rich fellowship with one another. They were bound together through their common goals and experiences.

Today the group has maintained a connection, though the connection is not as close as it was during the journey. Some of the families have been back to adopt again—but they went with other groups and formed other fellowships. While their original fellowship has parted, it has not been broken. Nothing can remove the bond they formed while they traveled that path together.

When you find yourself a part of a fellowship, explore it to the fullest. Don't sit in your room and isolate yourself from the other members of the group. The more you invest in your fellowships, the richer you will be.

Fellowship as a Verb

Another meaning of fellowship is to have a friendly relationship with someone else. It sounds a bit archaic to our ears, but it is possible to fellowship with another person. That means to enjoy one another's presence and the unique contributions each brings to the party.

We most easily fellowship with people who are united with us in purpose and thought. Fellowship is that comfortable excitement that arises when we speak to like-minded people of the things we're most passionate about.

Do you have people with whom you can fellowship? Maybe you get together with those who love the same sports team you do, despite the fact that this is not that team's hometown (Go, Cowboys!). Maybe you have found people who share your political, philosophical, or spiritual beliefs. Maybe you get together once a year with those who labor in your craft but usually work alone. It's such a relief to talk with someone who understands where you're coming from.

When Frodo and Sam were ascending Mount Doom, they tried to remember the Shire. They thought of spring and harvest and their beloved homes. No one else for hundreds of leagues could truly understand what they were talking about or the feeling they were remembering, and that was what made the fellowship so sweet. Together, they could create a space where their mutual joy could exist. Were they separate, their private memories wouldn't have sustained them. Their fellowshipping brought the Shire to life.

Seek out those with whom you can fellowship. The Internet is, like a magical ring, capable of both good and evil. But one of its more helpful aspects is that it can bring together people of similar mind who might otherwise remain separated by distance, language, or national boundaries.

Rich fellowship is awaiting you. Find it, build it, and enjoy it.

Alliances

Hobbits do not enter into alliances lightly. Oh, they might temporarily ally with pipeweed growers in the Southfarthing to ensure delivery of the stuff to Hobbiton, or they might agree to do business with Big Folk in Bree, but such arrangements are prickly and uneasy. It's hard to maintain permanent working relations with strangers who are so odd.

As for alliance with those outside of the Shire, should anyone be so foolish as to consider it, hobbits would be hard-pressed to find parties wanting to enter into such an arrangement. Hobbits are small, after all, even when compared to dwarves. No one comes to Bree looking to hire hobbit warriors or hobbit wizards or hobbit guides into Mordor. No one wants a hobbit army.

About the only thing outsiders might want from hobbits is pipeweed. It has been rumored that certain wizards have developed a taste for Old Toby.

Still, there are those who see the real value hobbits offer. Aside from the hardiness of certain Shirefolk, hobbits possess a simple enjoyment of life. Hobbits need no Rings of Power to be content. They need no dragon's hoard, no treasures of *mithril* or gold, no colossal palaces of stone. With good food, strong drink, and friends with whom to share them, a hobbit's life is complete.

Humans could learn a thing or two from hobbits.

Why did Strider and his Rangers keep diligent watch over the Shire? Why did they turn away creatures and shadows and unsavory elements? Why did Frodo and his friends remain in the War of the Ring when they could've come home? Why did a vision of Bag End in flames cause Frodo to plunge more deeply into his purpose?

It was to preserve that simple contentment that hobbits exude. It was to allow those hairy-footed little people to go on enjoying their ease, blissfully ignorant of all those who protected them from hiding.

Whose innocence are you protecting? To what lengths do you go to make sure someone precious and perhaps small and weak is able to go on not worrying about the larger affairs of the world? When you bear that burden, you are being heroic.

What alliance could you make with those who bring you mirth? How might you contribute to someone's ability to inspire you with his life of contentment? How could you enter into someone's *joie de vivre* and thus have it rub off on you?

As for making alliances as a hobbit might, you must consider what can you offer someone else to bring you what you need. Were a hobbit lord to seek an alliance with someone, he or she would likely try to find an army that could protect the Shire, a wizard who could guide it, dwarves who might build for it, and elves who might teach it the secrets of making. In return, you could provide song and joy (and pipeweed) and fellowship.

You do have much to offer, whether or not your finances are depleted. Others might be enriched by your personality, wisdom, and expertise. Who might benefit from what you can give? What part-nerships can you find that might benefit both parties, each supply-ing what the other lacks? Find the win-win scenarios around you, and win.

Conclusion

So what do you think: Hobbits for your fellowship? An alliance with the mighty diminutives? While you're deciding, walk into The Prancing Pony—they serve both Shirefolk and Big Folk there—and lift a pint with any hobbits you can find. As friends in the moment and friends in need, there are none better.

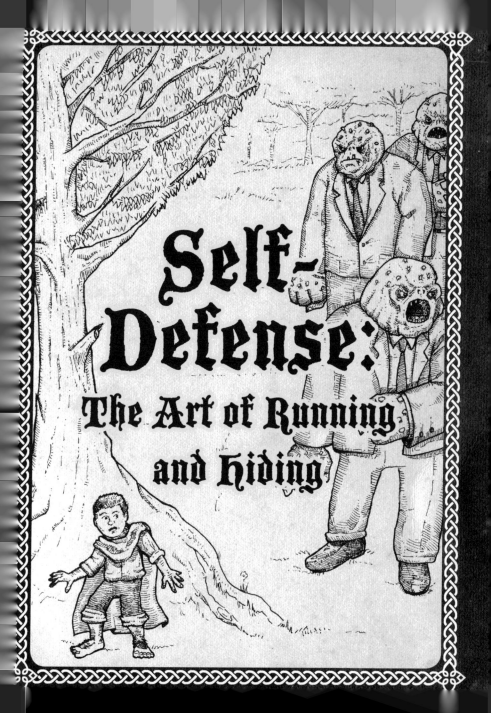

Self-Defense:
The Art of Running and Hiding

hey possessed from the first the art of disappearing swiftly and silently, when large folk whom they do not wish to meet come blundering by; and this art they have developed until to Men it may seem magical.

—From JRR Tolkien's
The Fellowship of the Ring

A Hobbit's Guide to Self-Defense

Hobbits are small creatures. They are not very aggressive. They are kindhearted, friendly, and sensitive. All of the wonderful things that make a hobbit a hobbit also put them in danger from other species of Middle-earth, who aren't as, well, nice. In *The Hobbit* and *The Lord of the Rings*, hobbits face a whole host of nasty creatures: trolls, goblins, wolves, spiders, dragons, orcs, Gollum, Ringwraiths, the dark wizard Saruman, and the dark lord Sauron, among others.

Hobbits have quite a few traits that are advantages as well, though you wouldn't necessarily think so by looking at them. Hobbits have thick pads on the soles of their feet (and no need for shoes), allowing them to tread quickly, lightly, and silently. Their bodies are small and quite fast, able to duck into tight places in order to evade predators. Hobbits are very comfortable in underground places—after all, they live in holes—so caverns and tunnels are no problem for hobbits and make great places for them to hide.

In addition to being able to quickly run and hide, hobbits are also quite cunning and quick-witted. When in danger they are usually able to come up with some pretty creative ways to find safety.

When forced to fight, hobbits can be as fierce as any small creature, particularly when defending a friend. However, they tend to use violence only as a last resort, opting to avoid danger whenever possible, which isn't a bad principle to live by ... not at all.

Running

Despite having short legs, hobbits can run rather quickly and will usually choose to do so rather than resort to violence. When trapped in the goblin tunnels with Gollum, Bilbo could have easily killed the creature with his sword but instead used his quick little legs to run at Gollum and jump over him. Of course, having gained invisibility from the Ring of Power helped a little bit, as well.

Running is often one of the best ways to keep oneself safe. While some people say that running away is a cowardly act, that is not necessarily the case. Standing and fighting just to fight isn't smart—especially if you are at a size disadvantage or facing an armed enemy. Plus, even if you win a fight you could be wounded, so there is often a price to pay. It's best to run away, period.

Running Techniques

When determining your running techniques, it's important to consider your body size, the length of your legs, the terrain, and the distance to safety. Hobbits are small but capable of running quickly over short distances, and they are also good at zigging and zagging. It's important to realize your own physical attributes and take them into account for your strategy of running and evading. If you are taller and have longer legs, you may want to run with longer strides (like an elf would), focusing on outpacing your enemy. If you are shorter, you'd do well to employ a hobbit's strategy of dodging and darting from side to side as you run.

A Hobbit's Advantage

As mentioned previously, hobbits have thick pads on the bottoms of their feet which allow them to run barefoot. While resistant to heat, cold, and injury, their feet still feel the terrain as they run. The connection to their terrain gives them greater mobility and the ability to run very quietly.

Luckily, with today's advances in technology, you can mimic the experience of running like a hobbit. Runners today can purchase a "barefoot"-style running shoe with toes. These shoes allow your toes to function as they should while you run. In other words, your feet work inside the shoe as they would naturally. And that's about as close to running like a hobbit as you can get!

When Not to Run

Running can save your life. There are times, however, when running is inappropriate. For instance, you should never run from something worth defending. A hobbit never abandons his friends and neither should you. Bilbo somehow found the courage to launch an attack against the spiders who were planning to eat his friends. Frodo threw himself into battle in the Mines of Moria when his friends were being attacked. Hobbits fight when they need to.

You may also find yourself trapped, and running may not be an option. If so, you will obviously want to employ another tactic, perhaps one of those that follow.

Hiding

Hiding is another act that some think cowardly but may actually save your life. Small creatures, such as hobbits, frequently hide out of necessity since many enemies are larger and more powerful than they are. A fight would hardly be fair. Hiding may allow you to conserve energy for later in battle, and if you're lucky you may avoid the conflict altogether.

Holes and Other Tight Places

Holes are a hobbit's best friend when danger arises. Holes may be dark and a bit frightening, but when your option is facing a powerful enemy it may be wise to consider overcoming your claustrophobic tendencies, squeeze into a tight place, and hide.

Hobbits feel right at home in tight places. Tunnels, caves, caverns, nooks, and crannies are not unlike their hobbit holes, so sneaking around in the dark in small spaces is not unfamiliar to them. Because of this they are able to keep their calm and their sense of direction even when finding their way through dark goblin tunnels. One can use small, dark spaces to their advantage as long as one keeps their wits about them. Creeping through tunnels quietly is a great way to avoid confrontations and, if necessary, may allow one to sneak up on an enemy.

Taking Cover

It's important to know when to take cover. When Bilbo and the dwarves found themselves under attack from the dragon Smaug, they hid inside a tunnel that led deep into the dragon's lair. The dwarves were hesitant to close the door, which they feared would lock them inside, but at the very last moment Bilbo convinced them to do so, thus saving them from Smaug's dreadful fire. You may not like where you have to hide, and your choices of cover may be limited, but it is part of having an adventure. Keep your head down, and do so quickly.

Safe Havens

Whenever you find yourself swept up in a nasty adventure or quest, it's good to know places where you may stay with friends or keep a low profile. Busy taverns or inns make great places for lying low (plus, when caught up in a bit of adventure, one could likely do with a nice hot meal or a pint of something strong to take the edge off).

Tolkien's adventurers often sought sanctuary with friends. For example, in Rivendale they stayed with the elf king Elrond, who pro-

vided lodgings, food, advice, and aid. Know your safe havens and
use them.

Camouflage

Never underestimate the usefulness of camouflage. In the film
The Return of the King, when Frodo and Sam were sneaking into
Mordor, they used an elvish cloak to hide amongst the rocks. Hobbits are also good at "disappearing" when in the forest. Study your
surroundings and learn how to blend in. Employ the use of specialized clothing or use materials around you (such as leaves or mud) to
disguise yourself. Sometimes hiding in plain sight is the best way
to hide.

Stealth

Hobbits can be quite stealthy when they want to (even without the aid
of an invisibility ring). Being a small creature gives you plenty of practice sneaking about, and hobbits have all sorts of clever ideas on how
to remain unseen. For example, when Bilbo's dwarf friends were captured by the Wood-elves, Bilbo devised an elaborate escape plan in
which the dwarves hid themselves in empty wine barrels that shipped
downriver to Lake-town in the south for reuse, as per the elves regular procedure. Not only were they able to escape but they also came
to a good place for the next phase of their journey to the dragon's lair.
You never know when you may find yourself in a situation where you
need to travel unseen. Study the lay of the land, the local routines
and procedures, and an idea such as Bilbo's barrel-riding plan may
present itself.

Avoiding

Say what you will, but avoiding something is often the very
best way to stay out of harm's way. Hobbits are brilliant avoiders.
They can come up with innumerable excuses for staying out
of adventure—and you can rest assured that each and every one

of their excuses will sound quite sensible if you take the time to consider it.

Staying Home

The best way to hide is to stay home. Period. Many times during his adventures, Bilbo wished he was back in his snug little hobbit hole sitting by the hearth. He dreamt of bacon and eggs and bread and butter and piping hot tea. Your home is likely the best place to avoid trouble. Sometimes, however, trouble comes to you—as it did with Frodo. The Nazgul—also known as Ringwraiths or dark riders—were drawn to the Ring, which came into Frodo's possession. The Shire would have been in danger had Frodo not undertaken his quest to carry the Ring away from his village. So, as good as it may sound, staying home isn't always an option.

Strength in Numbers

A particularly effective way to avoid danger is the old adage of finding strength in numbers. Aside from simply loving to have company, hobbits always keep companions near in times of trouble. Both *The Hobbit* and *The Lord of the Rings* illustrate the importance of strength in numbers. At the start of *The Hobbit*, Bilbo is conscripted into an adventure because the dwarves are seeking another member. They need to add to their troupe so they'll have a lucky number. In *The Lord of the Rings*, when Frodo is charged with the task of carrying the Ring of Power, all of his friends understand the task is his and his alone. Only Frodo can carry the Ring, but his friends won't let him undertake the journey alone. They form the Fellowship of the Ring to accompany him on his quest. One of the great messages in all of Tolkien's work is that of friendship and loyalty. A fellowship, such as the Fellowship of the Ring, is the very definition of strength in numbers.

Wit and Cunning

Hobbits can be quick thinkers and are also bookworms, so their heads are full of all kinds of forgotten facts and stories. When Bilbo was trapped in the dark with Gollum, he used a game of riddles to distract the creature so he could escape. Later, when he was confronted by the dragon Smaug, he employed more riddles and good manners to stall for time. You'd be surprised what a hobbit might think of in a pinch. Their quick wits have been known to help them out of many a dangerous situation.

Disguise

Wearing a disguise is a great way to avoid capture or harm. When Frodo and Sam sneak through the Black Gate of Mordor, they wear orcish armor. This tactic can prove quite effective. If you are able to acquire enemy clothing or armor, it's the next best thing to having a Ring of Power. You'll be invisible (and without the annoying side effect of turning evil).

Protective Clothing

A shirt made of *mithril*, a priceless, lightweight metal mined by dwarves, saved Frodo's life on several occasions. The shirt, part of the treasure retrieved from Smaug's horde, was given to Frodo by Bilbo, who wore it during the Battle of the Five Armies.

If you know you are going to be in a dangerous situation, then wearing some sort of armor is a good precaution to take. Whether tall boots for warding off snakes in a swamp or a Kevlar vest on the wrong side of town, the right protective clothing can mean the difference between life and death.

Finding the Enemy's Weakness

The second time Bilbo sneaked into Smaug's lair he found himself noticed by the awakened dragon despite having worn his invisibility ring. Bilbo was forced to stall for time and speak to the worm (which is what they sometimes called dragons) in riddles. Though in danger

of being pulled under Smaug's powerful influence, Bilbo managed to keep his wits about him and tricked the dragon into revealing a weak spot in his underbelly.

Every enemy has some weakness. The trick is to carefully research your enemy or perform reconnaissance in order to find out what the weakness is. You may be taking a risk, but you may also uncover information that will help you win the battle in the long run.

Words as Self-Defense

Often the best way out of a jam is simply to talk your way out of it. Bilbo used this tactic on several occasions. When the trolls debate whether to put him in a stew pot, Bilbo reasons with them, telling them that he would be much more useful as a cook than a meal. His doing so stalls things long enough for Gandalf to rescue him. When trapped with Gollum in the goblin tunnels, Bilbo used a game of riddles to bargain with the creature. Gollum agreed to show Bilbo the way out if Bilbo won the game. When confronted by Smaug, Bilbo relied on conversation as well. Simply talking with an opponent can often delay or diffuse a tense situation, or you may be able to discover valuable information that you may use later.

Fighting Back

While it's best to avoid violence, sometimes no matter what you do, you are headed for an unavoidable conflict and you'll be forced to fight back. In those instances, it's important to know some strategy and technique for surviving a battle.

Battle Cries

While hobbits may not think of themselves as having a battle cry, they are capable of very loud and startling sounds when under duress. When Bilbo was surprised by lightning generated by Gandalf's magic staff, he emitted a shrill noise that froze all thirteen dwarves in their tracks. Employing such a tactic in a self-defense situation may prove quite effective in distracting one's enemy and providing a window of opportunity. A battle cry may seem a little dramatic and silly to one who has never had the occasion to use it. However, the battle cry can serve many purposes in a fight or self-defense situation. A battle cry can also startle an opponent, giving one an opportunity to escape or launch a counterattack. Moreover, in martial arts the battle cry is often used in coordination with a technique in order to focus power, much in the same way one groans when lifting a heavy object.

On the Battlefield

Assuming one finds oneself on a field of battle, it likely means one has been swept up in some sort of nasty adventure, and there is a lot to consider. First, it's important to focus on the moment at hand. Concerns for your own safety and that of others must be set aside temporarily. Survival counts on your ability to react quickly, and you must focus solely on what is happening around you so you can rely on all your talents. Hobbits are quick on their feet and are good at hiding, ducking, evading, and wiggling into and out of tight spots. These are all good tactics to employ—an evasive strategy can serve you well. However, one must also consider the reason one is in battle in the first place. If your goal is to protect your friends, you must find your courage and pick opportune moments to stand your ground and engage your enemy. Bilbo, for example, never would have imagined himself in battle. Yet, when his friends were tangled in webs and in danger of being eaten by giant spiders, he devised a clever plan of attack that involved throwing stones and taunting the spiders to draw them away long enough for him to free his friends.

Unarmed Tactics

Due to their small size, hobbits have to get creative when it comes to self-defense. When attacked by large enemies, they are forced to take advantage of whatever vulnerable areas are within reach. This includes knees, toes, ankles, shins, and the groin. Humans might consider the striking of some of these areas to be "fighting dirty," however, when one is in a self-defense situation it is important to make use of any target of opportunity. A swift kick to the shin or a sharp punch to the groin may save your life. If, unlike hobbits, you have the advantage of height, other good targets include the eyes and the throat.

Kicking

Kicks are great self-defense techniques for hobbits, as hobbits possess incredibly tough feet. But even if you don't have hobbit feet, a well-placed kick can save your life. There are various kicks you can employ that will work against an attacker of any size.

- **STOMP KICK:** This kick is delivered with either a downward motion (which is great for stomping on an enemy's foot) or by raising your knee high and pushing your foot forward into an attacker's midsection. This kick can be delivered with great force and makes it an excellent choice for stopping an attacker.

- **FRONT KICK:** Similar to the second variety of stomp kick, but instead of a pushing motion, the kick is delivered more quickly and sharply. Pull your toes back and use the ball of your foot as the striking surface. This kick can be very effective for targeting a shin, the groin, or the abdomen.

- **SIDEKICK:** This kick is delivered by pivoting on your standing foot and shooting your leg out sideways toward your attacker. Extend your heel forward as you kick. A well-placed sidekick can cause severe damage to an attacker's knee.

- **ROUND HOUSE:** Lift your knee and then swing your leg across your body like a club or a baseball bat. You can strike using your foot or your shin, depending on your attacker's distance. This is the fastest kick to execute, so it's a good choice for quick deployment.

- **BACK KICK:** Do this kick correctly and you'll be able to kick your enemy like a mule. Perfect for an attacker that sneaks up behind you, a back kick is executed by looking over one's shoulder and kicking straight back with the heel of the foot extended. Aim for a larger part of the body, such as the mid-section, as this kick is a bit more difficult to perform with great accuracy.

Hand Techniques

Punches and other strikes with the hand aren't quite as effective for hobbits, given their small size. But, no matter your size, it's good to know a few techniques in case a target of opportunity presents itself.

- **PUNCH:** A punch is delivered with a closed fist. Make sure your fingers are curled tightly with your thumb on the outside. As you punch, extend through the shoulder to get the best reach and deliver the most force. If you're short like a hobbit, aim for the groin. If you're taller, aim for the face or throat. And a gut shot works no matter how tall you are.

- **PALM STRIKE:** Similar to a punch, the palm strike is delivered with open fingers and the heel of the hand. Remember to keep your thumb tucked in so it doesn't snag on clothing (or armor).

- **CHOP:** A strike delivered with the edge of the hand in a down-ward motion. Hobbits have the opportunity to use this when an attacker picks them up (which, come to think of it, happens a lot). A good target for the chop is the neck.

- **EYE GOUGE:** Also a good technique to employ when an enemy picks you up. Just stick your finger or thumb right in his eye and he'll set you down straightaway.

The Element of Surprise

Using the element of surprise in battle can be very effective. Catch-ing an enemy off guard can provide a few extra seconds, which may be just the amount of time you need in order to escape (or launch an attack). The element of surprise worked in Bilbo's favor when he was fleeing the goblin's cave. Suddenly he found himself face-to-face with a group of goblins, but he quickly slipped the ring of invisibility onto his finger, rushed passed them, and squeezed through a small crack in the door and into the sunlight. The goblins saw his shadow, but they were so startled they didn't have much chance to give chase. Bilbo got away with a loss of only a few buttons from his jacket.

Weapons

Hobbits don't typically use weapons; when they do, they normally use a gardening implement or a broom (which can be quite effective for smacking an enemy over the head or at the knees). When occasions demand it, however, hobbits have been known to take up arms. Both Bilbo and Frodo carried an elvish blade they called Sting. While actually a dagger, Sting was the perfect size for a hobbit to use as a sword. This is a great example to keep in mind when choosing a weapon; you want to arm yourself with a weapon appropriate to your size. You want something you can wield effectively. If you're small in build, for example, don't run out and buy a .44 magnum for home defense. (Actually, no one should have a .44 magnum for home defense, no matter their size.)

Swords

Swords in the works of Tolkien are more than just weapons. They often have a significance beyond just being a blade. Bilbo's sword Sting (later passed to Frodo), along with other elvish swords, would glow blue in the presence of goblins or orcs. Many of the swords of Middle-earth had names such as Orcrist (the Goblin-cleaver) and Glamdring (the Foe-hammer).

Swords aren't often used today. When they are, they likely have a more symbolic meaning similar to the meaning these special blades had in Tolkien's works. For example, consider the significance of the calvary swords awarded to United States Marines. These blades are more a symbol of honor than a weapon meant to be used practically in battle.

Axes

The battle-axe is a weapon often used by dwarves in Tolkien's works. This heavy weapon isn't much use to a small hobbit, but for someone large enough to wield one, a battle-axe can make quite an impression on your enemy—oh wait, make that two half-enemies.

Makeshift Weapons

Almost anything can be used as a weapon in a time of need. A simple stick, for example, can be used as a staff—and while it likely won't be capable of magic like Gandalf's staff, it will still be quite good for knocking an enemy on the head.

Long Distance Weapons

Keeping your distance from your enemy is always a good idea when possible. Bilbo threw rocks at the spiders that had captured his friends. Rocks can be great weapons for striking an opponent from a distance or for causing a diversion that can let you employ a secondary attack or escape.

Elves are fond of using bows and arrows. This is an excellent long-distance weapon—just consider the sheer number of orcs laid to waste by Legolas in *The Lord of the Rings*.

Other long-distance weapons include spears, which can be thrown (not often very accurately), crossbows (not as easy to reload as a bow and arrow but more powerful), and catapults (which are rarely something one would have in a self-defense scenario and effective only when you are stationary—good for an initial barrage, but after that, you will need to find something else).

Mercy

Of course, with all of this talk about tactics, let's return to the fact that hobbits abhore violence. Whenever there is an alternative to combat, they will almost always choose a nonviolent course of action. In the heat of battle one should try to remember one's morals and exercise good judgment and mercy. Remember to only use violence when necessary or called for, especially when you have the upper hand. For example, when Bilbo was trapped in the goblin cave with the creature Gollum, he was armed with his sword and wearing the Ring of Power, which made him invisible. It would have been easy for Bilbo to kill Gollum then and there. But instead, Bilbo pitied the creature and simply sneaked past him to escape. Ask yourself: What would you have done?

A Hobbit's Guide to Monsters

With all this talk of self-defense—running, hiding, fighting back, and the like—you may be asking yourself, "Yes, this is all well and good, but should I know more specifically about these trolls, orcs, wolves, and other assorted beasties? And should special considerations be taken in the event of encountering certain nasty creatures?"

In a word, yes. Here are some descriptions of the various monstrosities you may run into in Middle-earth, and advice on what to do when dealing with them.

Spiders (and Assorted Bugs)

Almost every creature is scarier if it's larger. If we hear a scratching at the door, open it, and find a ten-foot-tall cockroach, we scream. The next time we open the door (assuming we're still around to do so) and find a hundred-foot-tall cockroach, we scream even louder. Scale has a lot to do with the power to frighten, especially when what we're meeting is something that in ordinary life isn't much bigger than a quarter (or possibly a half-dollar).

Bilbo and Frodo run into various spiders as they adventure their way through Middle-earth, ranging from the large to the small.

Small Bugs and Spiders

When, under the prodding of the dwarves in the middle of Mirkwood, Bilbo climbs a tree to see if he can find out how much farther the party has to go, he worries all the way up about what he'll do if he encounters large spiders. Fortunately, the ones he meets prove to be only the ordinary size, and he ignores them. He also meets large black velvet butterflies, which only flap about his head. He safely discounts them. Even at night, when the dwarves' campfire brings moths "as big as your hand," Bilbo is more irritated than frightened. The rule of thumb, then, is that as long as insects are the normal size, you can squish them without problem.

Sleeping in the open, you'll probably encounter this issue more often than you'd like. Bugs like the warmth the human body provides, and they're quite likely to cluster around you in your sleep, seeking out especially your hair (including whatever hair you have on your feet) and crevices in your clothing. Rise several times during the night and shake yourself thoroughly to rid yourself of the pests. If you come to a place of shelter such as Rivendell or an inn, a hot bath and thorough soaping is recommended, including carefully washing your hair and rinsing it to delouse yourself.

Keep in mind that spiders of the small variety are generally useful, at least in gardens. They eat garden pests and keep plants free from disease. Giant spiders don't work on the same principle, but there's no reason to take out your frustration about large spiders on their normal-sized relatives.

Larger Spiders

The giant spiders of Mirkwood are thoroughly nasty and apt to eat anything that falls into their webs. They take their time about it, preferring to let their meat hang a bit (head downward, if possible) in order to properly age it. To avoid them, take the following steps:

- **STAY ON THE FREAKING PATH!** It's protected by magic, you've been told it's protected by magic, and you've seen abundant evidence that the wood is filled with all sorts of other nasty creatures that don't attack you as long as you stay on the path. So stay on the path and don't stray! What's the matter with you, anyway?

- **FIRE CAN BE YOUR FRIEND.** It's true that it attracts all sorts of eyes, including "bulbous insect eyes," but it also scares spiders (and quite possibly other creatures). Keep a fire going at night, and keep a close watch so it doesn't go out.
- **HAVE PLENTY OF STONES HANDY.** A well-thrown stone can take out a spider, knocking it unconscious or even dead.
- **IN THE EVENT OF A SPIDER ATTACK, STAY TOGETHER, THROW STONES, AND USE YOUR SWORDS TO CUT THROUGH THE WEBS AS THEY'RE STRUNG AROUND YOU.** Mobility is your greatest advantage, so try to move back to the path, where its magic will protect you. What's that? You don't have swords? Then you shouldn't be adventuring in the first place!
- **SPIDERS ARE HIGHLY TERRITORIAL AND WON'T WILLINGLY VENTURE OUT OF PLACES THEY CONTROL.** They also don't like elf magic, since the elves of Mirkwood are constantly killing them and otherwise annoying them. So if you know of a place in Mirkwood where elves have been recently, head for it. The spiders are unlikely to follow you there.
- **PRACTICE YOUR NAME CALLING.** For some reason, spiders seem more sensitive to this than most other creatures. (There is no recorded instance of orcs being upset by hobbits or anyone else calling them "ugly, stinky, big-headed, long-armed, foul-bodied booger faces.") If you can throw off attacking spiders by yelling names at them, you've got a strategic advantage you can play to the hilt. Use Bilbo's song for inspiration:

> Bilbo, however, soon slipped away to a different place. The idea came to him to lead the furious spiders further and further away from the dwarves, if he could; to make them curious, excited and angry all at once. When about fifty had gone off to the place where he had stood before, he threw some more stones at these, and at others that had stopped behind; then dancing among the trees he began to sing a song to infuri-

ate them and bring them all after him, and also to let the dwarves hear
his voice.

This is what he sang:

Old fat spider spinning in a tree!
Old fat spider can't see me!
Attercop! Attercop!
Won't you stop,
Stop your spinning and look for me?

Old Tomnoddy, all big body,
Old Tomnoddy, can't spy me!
Attercop! Attercop!
Down you drop!
You'll never catch me up your tree! (*The Hobbit*, chapter 8)

Giant Spiders

To be honest, there's really only one completely giant spider in
Middle-earth, and that's Shelob, who inhabits the pass near Cirith
Ungol in the Mountains of Shadow on the borders of Mordor. There
are stories of others, starting with the great spider Ungoliant,
but you're not likely to encounter them. You're not all that likely
to encounter Shelob either, if you stay away from Mordor, which
would be a good idea. If, however, you run into her, remember
the following:

- **SHE'S NOT AS STRONG AS SHE USED TO BE.** She lost one
  eye in an encounter with Samwise Gamgee, and her legs are
  scarred, so she can't move quite as quickly as formerly. Stay
  on her blind side, and slash at her legs. If possible, take out
  the other eye.
- **HER UNDERBELLY IS ANOTHER WEAK SPOT.** She's been
  stabbed there once before; bonus points to you if you can cut
  her there again.
- **IF, IN RUNNING THROUGH HER TUNNELS, YOU ENCOUNTER VIC-
  TIMS WHOM SHE'S COVERED IN WEBS AND HUNG FOR LATER**

MEALS, KEEP MOVING. It's very unlikely you'll be able to cut them free in time to escape, and even if you did, they've been poisoned, so you'll wind up carrying them, which will only slow you down. Just keep moving. Think of yourself. This is no time for bravery.

· **SHELOB (AND MOST LARGE SPIDERS) IS HIGHLY SENSITIVE TO SUDDEN, BRIGHT LIGHT.** Bring along a strong light source, say, a magical light given to you by the elves, one that you've forgotten about until the absolute last minute of fighting with Shelob—and you can intimidate her and make her back off long enough to escape.

· **REMEMBER THAT SHELOB IS NEUTRAL TO ANY CONFLICT BETWEEN YOU AND ASSORTED ORCS YOU MAY HAVE RUN INTO.** If a party of orcs is chasing you, leading them into Shelob's lair may be a strategically useful move. At least you can count on her to take out four or five of them (assuming, of course, that you can escape her clutches first).

Wolves

Wolves are nasty because they can run faster than you, are probably stronger than you, and hunt in packs, therefore outnumbering you. You have the advantage of reason and intelligence, but that's a small comfort when you're stuck on a lonely hillside in the middle of the night, listening to the howls of hungry wolves.

Ordinary Wolves

Normal, everyday wolves aren't so bad. Even though they're often hungry, they tend not to attack people, and if they do, they can be easily intimidated by fire, arrows, and a few beheadings via dwarvish axes. In fact, it's possible to capture wolf cubs and train them to be useful. Nonetheless, meeting a pack of wolves in the Wild, the sensible adventurer should seek the high ground and find something to throw to the wolves to satisfy their hunger: spare food, the superfluous hobbit....

Fire Is Your Friend

Wolves don't like fire; its sparks burn them and can even set them ablaze. Also, they don't like light. If you find yourself on a hill top with old trees, try setting them on fire. For spectacular effects, set them on fire with a big blast of magic. If the wolves are ordinary wolves—and you certainly hope they are—they'll run away with their tails between their legs.

Wargs

Wargs are wolves that owe a special allegiance to Mordor and its Dark Lord. They often ally with goblins or orcs, and they've been known to hunt with their allies. Although they're generally found on the west side of the Anduin, in times of crisis they cross the river.

Wargs are large (usually the size of small horses), heavy, and have long teeth, used to rip and tear their victims' flesh. Their fur is coarse and resistant to sword blows and axe strokes. They can be killed with arrows from a distance, but their speed makes them difficult targets. The orcs who ride them can make them a double threat.

The best course, when you see a group of orc-ridden wargs racing down the hillside toward you, is to make a stand. If you have mounted people in your party, you may decide to stage a charge to break the wargs' momentum. In hand-to-hand combat, aim for the throats and legs, which are the most vulnerable parts. Try to avoid having a warg fall on top of you—they're heavy, especially in death.

Wargs don't like fire (see above), and if you have a wizard in the party (always an excellent idea), he may be able to kindle some magic flames to set them ablaze. Pine cones make good missiles in this sort of defense.

Wargs have a language of sorts, and they can speak Goblin—at least enough to communicate on a rudimentary level. Learning a bit of Warg and Goblin might come in handy; it will give you the advantage of anticipating your enemies' attacks and plans.

Goblins and Orcs

Goblins, hobgoblins, and orcs are all more or less the same types of creature. They were created from elves by the Enemy in the early days of Middle-earth. Today they're built on an assembly-line principle, hatched out of some mysterious magical process, with other orcs present to attach the fins and fog lights at the last minute. During the War of the Ring, the fallen wizard Saruman came up with a method of building orcs who could withstand the rays of the sun, even at noon (though they still didn't like the Evil Orb of Day very much). Apart from these sun-resistant models, orcs and goblins generally don't like daylight; it makes them weak and dizzy and gives them headaches.

Goblins

Goblins inhabit mountains, where they live in caves. They emerge to raid passing parties of travelers. They're armed mostly with swords (usually with crooked blades) and spears. They eat ponies, as well as the passing dwarf, minced, sautéed, and in a sauce. (They're unacquainted with cooking hobbit, but only because of a lack of opportunity; they'd love to try it.)

Goblins are generally stupid and highly dependent on authority. When Gandalf manages to kill the Great Goblin, the rest of the entourage goes to pieces, allowing the dwarves, hobbit, and wizard to escape into the tunnels beneath the Misty Mountains. However, goblins have a highly developed sense of direction, especially in their own dwellings, and they can move silently—more silently, at any rate, than dwarves.

If you're attacked by goblins, your best bet is to kill whoever is in authority and get away in the ensuing confusion. If you sense you're being followed, you probably are, in which case you may as well stand and fight. Goblins are the red shirts of the adventuring world: They're easily disposed of, but it doesn't matter how many you kill; there are always more of them.

Bolg the Goblin

Bolg was the leader of the goblin armies during the Battle of Five Armies. He and his family had a long history of conflict with the dwarves. Bolg's father, Azog, conquered Moria and killed Thror, Thorin Oakenshield's grandfather. To take revenge, Thráin, Thror's son, attacked Moria in alliance with other dwarf tribes. One of the leaders of these tribes, Náin of the Iron Hills, challenged Azog to single combat before the gates of Moria. Azog and he fought, until finally Azog kicked Náin's legs from under him and with a single great stroke broke the dwarf's neck. In anger, Náin's son, Dáin, leaped up the steps and caught Azog. Right before the gates of Moria, he hewed off the goblin's head, thus avenging his father. To avenge this death (goblins, like dwarves, are big on vengeance), Bolg launched the attack on the Lonely Mountain that led to the Battle of Five Armies. But the plan backfired when Beorn appeared during the battle and fought his way through the bodyguard of Bolg, pulled down the goblin, and crushed him to death.

Hobgoblins

Hobgoblins are like goblins, only they come in the large economy size. They're found especially in the north in the Grey Mountains, but you can encounter them in other mountain ranges as well. Most of them were killed or scattered in the Battle of Five Armies, but since then they've had a chance to re-create themselves. (Incidentally, part of the proof that goblins and their ilk are created rather than bred is that we never hear about female goblins or orcs, or little orcklings, for that matter.)

The same general principles for fighting goblins apply to their larger cousins, hobgoblins. Disrupt the chain of command and you have a good chance of victory. Hobgoblins are harder to kill because of their size; the bodyguard of Bolg was made up of such creatures (see above). To defeat hobgoblins, it helps to have allies of similar stature—for instance a giant were-bear.

Orcs

Orcs are the shock troops of the Dark Tower, and Mordor is filled with them. Sauron doesn't care about them; they're completely expendable, and there's no sign that he's especially upset or discouraged by their deaths at the Battle of Helms Deep or the Battle of the Pelennor Fields. Because they're corrupt, they're entirely bad; there's no such thing as a redeemable orc or an orc with a conscience.

Orcs come in several varieties:

- **LARGE ORCS WITH SHUFFLING GATE AND LONG ARMS, HANGING ALMOST TO THEIR SIDES.** They have tusks as well as teeth, which they can use to rip and tear at their foes. They wear varying degrees of armor, depending on the company to which they belong—usually breastplates, shin guards, and helmets. These larger orcs are the commanders, and they keep their positions by killing anyone or anything that gets in their way. The result is that leadership in a company of orcs is a fluid, shifting business, with the top orcs constantly getting killed off by those striving for promotion.

  Orcs of all types travel in packs—it's rare to meet an isolated orc. The leaders maintain strict discipline with the liberal use of whips or, occasionally, by lopping off a few heads by way of example. There is competition between the companies of orcs to see who can be strongest, meanest, and most fanatical in their devotion to the Dark Lord; so when two companies meet, look for fights to break out.

- **MEDIUM ORCS.** These are the most common breed, used for everything from assaulting a fortress to guarding a prisoner. They're bulky, stupid, and generally obedient, at least up to the point that they're supplied with food and drink. Starve an orc and create a rebellion, as orc commanders are wont to say. (Needless to say, orcs are never so much at one another's throats that they won't drop all their quarrels in the face of a common enemy, such as an elf, a dwarf, a man, or a halfling.

It's a very bad idea to bank too much on divisions within orc forces. They're temporary and don't mean much in the long run.) In addition to foot soldiers, these orcs are also used in construction projects, such as building and maintaining the road between the Dark Tower and Mount Doom—or, for that matter, building the Dark Tower itself.

- **SMALLER ORCS, USED AS TRACKERS.** These have broad noses with wide nostrils, helpful in sniffing out scents. They're held in contempt by larger orcs, but they're still useful and thus immune to an extent from the normal process of self-elimination that distinguishes others of this race.

Uruk-hai

These are the orcs made by Saruman, possibly by blending humans and orcs. They're bigger and stronger than most other orcs and, most important, they can function even in full sunlight (though they prefer the dark). They're also extremely good at endurance races; if the orcs held a marathon, these guys would win it hands down. As far as food and drink go, they eat dried meat and drink water—but they're not especially particular about where the meat comes from. Humans, dwarves, elves, and hobbits are all possible sources of food.

Orcs in Battle

Orcs have no real sense of tactics or strategy; their preferred method of fighting is the straight-on attack, relying on superiority of numbers. Their weak wills allow them to be easily controlled by the Dark Lord and his minions.

When they're wounded, they either lie patiently, waiting for someone to kill them, or, if the wound isn't serious, they can cure it. This they do with a foul-smelling unguent, smeared directly on the wound. It hurts a good deal, but it heals quickly, albeit with scars. Scars, however, don't matter to orcs; they rather covet them.

Evading Orcs

Orcs have a keen sense of smell, but their hearing isn't all that good, so your best method of hiding from them is to find a stream of water, walk down it for a ways to throw them off the scent, then climb a tree and stay very, very quiet.

Fighting Orcs

In battle, orcs are all about wild slashing, relying on numbers rather than skill at arms. Peppering them with arrows from a distance is safest, but a reasonably good swordsman can take down an orc. Even hobbits don't have a lot of trouble with this kind of combat, since most orcs (except for Uruk-hai) tend toward the short side.

Trolls

Several different kinds of trolls wander about the Wild (or under it), and the wary adventurer should know what to do with each in case of confrontation. The main difficulty with trolls lies in their strength and size, both of which are immense. Fortunately, all of that bone and muscle leaves astonishingly little room for brains, which is where you may emerge victorious from a conflict with one or more trolls.

Stone Trolls

Stone trolls are generally found in the mountains, but unlike their cousins, the cave trolls (see next page), stone trolls live outside rather than underground. However, because the sun will turn them to stone, they require a cave or hole to which they can retreat during the day, emerging only after sundown.

Stone trolls are generally about twelve to fifteen feet tall and strong in proportion. They eat whatever's available, including humans, animals, dwarves, and elves (and orc, when they can get it, although discerning trolls argue that orc meat is too tough for a satisfying dinner). They arm themselves with clubs, but other equipment can include knives, forks, iron pots (for boiling food), and whatever they can plunder from their victims.

Stone trolls steal gold and silver, though it's doubtful that they get much good from it, since they don't engage in trade or barter with anyone or anything.

Encountering a Stone Troll

Stone trolls may be strong but they're remarkably stupid, even for trolls. You can keep them occupied with clever word play, imitations, or conversation that goes just above their level of understanding—which is to say, barely on the edge of sentience. Keep this up long enough and the sun will peep over the horizon, turning them to stone. Alternatively, sneak up behind them and stab them with a knife or sword; something with a strong blade is advised, since troll skin is notoriously thick.

Troll Purses

Troll purses, as Bilbo learns to his cost, are mischievous and talkative. The best thing to do is stay well away from them. Resist any temptation to pick trolls' pockets, easy as such a task may seem. It's likely to cause more trouble than it's worth.

Cave Trolls

Cave trolls are less talkative and less mobile than stone trolls, living as they do in caves and mines. They often serve as the muscle for bands of goblins or orcs and are usually the first sent into situations that the latter consider dangerous; a troll, after all, can take a great deal of damage before falling.

The skin of cave trolls is even stronger than that of stone trolls, since they have to walk or crawl through the rough-hewn tunnels made by goblins. They can see a long way in the dark, characteristic of any creature of the underground realms, and they're peculiarly adept at squeezing into surprisingly small spaces in search of food. They eat anything that comes to hand, including grubs, bats, rats, adventurers, and goblins when they can get away with it.

Encountering a Cave Troll

Cave trolls are best attacked by a strong party of intrepid adventurers, heavily armed with swords, knives, axes, and a smattering of magic. The best course may be for the party's wizard to collapse the roof of a tunnel on the troll, being careful not to bring down the rest of the cave on the heads of his own party. Failing that, stab the troll in whatever vulnerable parts are exposed to view. When shooting arrows, aim for the eyes or neck. Cave trolls are afraid of fire and are blinded by its light, so if the party has torches, it will prove a valuable advantage.

Stone Giants

Stone giants are distant cousins of trolls—larger, even stupider, and somewhat rarer. They live in the upper reaches of mountain ranges and usually come out only during storms, when they like to hurl boulders at one another for amusement. They don't particularly hate travelers, but they're inclined to regard travelers as objects for target practice more than anything else. For this reason, they're best avoided. It's possible to come across a giant with more communication skills than usual. Such individuals can become useful allies.

Stone giants stand twenty or thirty feet tall—they have been recorded as high as forty feet—and broad in proportion. They live in shallow caves on the mountainside, and their skin so strongly resembles rock that parties of dwarves have been known to start excavating on them before realizing their mistake.

Balrogs

Balrogs are about the biggest, nastiest, most evil creatures to be found in Middle-earth, even worse than dragons. The reason for this is that they're fallen or corrupted maiar—the angelic spirits first created by the Valar. (Gandalf is a maiar, for example). Although much more numerous in the past (in old chronicles, there are references to armies of balrogs fighting on behalf of Morgoth), there are still a few of these terrible creatures, mostly found in isolated places in the world. They've largely gone to ground, but every now and then some idiotic adventurer stirs one up, usually with bad results for everyone, starting with the adventurer.

Balrogs are between twelve and twenty feet tall, dark, and winged, although it's not clear that the wings are much use to them, particularly since most of them live underground. No one has ever seen a flying balrog. They have manes of long hair and tend to catch fire easily, though since balrogs are a type of flame elemental, the fire doesn't harm them and is used by them as an offensive weapon. If, by some chance, their fire is extinguished, they become slimy, though they still retain their immense strength. Their weapons include swords and multi-stranded whips, also flaming.

Staying Away From Balrogs

Most balrogs have been destroyed or banished to the dark places of the world. If you want to avoid them, therefore, the best thing is to stay out of those dark places. The further down in a cavern complex you explore, the greater the chance of meeting one of these dreadful spirits. Some warning signs that you're getting close to balrog territory:

- The burned-out skeletons of adventurers sprawled in heaps on the ground
- Stones melted from immense heat
- Groups of orcs kneeling in worship before an unseen deity
- A broken bridge over a huge chasm, leading down into darkness (Note: You can find one of these in the Mines of Moria.)

Getting Away From Balrogs

If you have the bad luck to encounter a balrog, your best hope is to run. And run fast. In one-on-one combat you can't hope to defeat it; even a skilled wizard has only a fifty-fifty chance of victory. Different races may use different tactics in such circumstances:

- **MEN.** Run away. Even if you have a famous sword, run away. The balrog doesn't care about your famous sword. Its sword is

made of molten metal and can cut through your armor like butter. This is no time to be a hero. Just leave.

- **ELVES.** You say you want to shoot arrows at it. Sure. Go ahead.
  See all the good that's likely to do you. A balrog could look like
  a pincushion of arrows and it wouldn't even slow down. Don't
  waste your time with your bow; just run.
- **DWARVES.** You guys are the ones that stirred up the balrog in
  Moria, so you should know better than to stick around when it's
  chasing you. Get those short legs moving.
- **HOBBITS.** Are you kidding me? You guys wouldn't even be an
  appetizer for this creature. Run. Or better, have someone with
  more speed carry you.
- **WIZARDS.** Only the most powerful magic will work here, so if
  you aren't feeling up to par, join the rest of your companions in
  running away. If you're able to unleash a spell, do so with the
  appropriate flourishes. Balrogs are often intimidated by flashy
  magical effects. Giant sheets of flame or burning missiles are
  always good.

Dragons

Dragons were more numerous once than they are today, but even so
it's not unheard of to run into one now and again. They're attracted
by large hoards of treasure, as well as a sizeable food supply of villagers or countryfolk. Some dragons became legendary, while others
faded into obscurity and may still be hidden in caves on some distant
mountainside, waiting for the right moment to emerge.

Dragons are highly intelligent creatures with remarkable powers of conversation. They have the ability to charm their interlocutor
into revealing himself or at least revealing more information than
he intended about himself and his companions. Smaug is typical
of the breed—he speaks Common far more capably than any of the
other creatures Bilbo meets on his travels, and he has something of
a sense of humor.

On the other hand, dragons' intelligence can be a weakness. They can't resist riddling talk; they are fascinated by it and are willing to spend hours guessing at a riddle's meaning. They can overthink situations, and sometimes their intelligence makes them overconfident. A clever move on your part can send them off on the wrong scent entirely. Still, unless you're a wizard or have a good deal of experience dealing with dragons (and that's true of very few people), your best bet is to keep your chats with live dragons short, sweet, and to the point.

Dragons live an extremely long time—generally four or five hundred years, depending on food supply and whether anyone shoots magical arrows at them. This being the case, they have long memories and a taste for revenge, not only against the person who injured them but against his descendants and his descendants' descendants. On the whole, therefore, it's bad practice to make an enemy of a dragon. But sometimes it just can't be avoided.

Types of Dragons

Varying types of dragons exist, and each type requires a different combat strategy and differing times for a head start in running away. It should be noted, though, that all dragons have in common their love of precious things and their remarkable ability to keep an exact accounting of all items in their hoard and their current market value. This is not to mention the fact that dragon hoards are vast beyond imagination, each containing hundreds, if not thousands, of items stolen over the years from hapless kings and emperors. Thus, burgling a dragon's treasure has got to be one of the stupidest enterprises ever conceived by the mind of a dwarf—in this case, Thorin Oakenshield.

Fire Dragons

These are the most common wyrms. Their size ranges from 150 feet to 300 feet, snout to tail. Their often-immense size makes them intimidating, but it also makes it somewhat difficult for them to hide themselves, and sooner or later some busybody of a hero is likely to come bounding into their lair, waving a big magic sword and declaring his intention of cooking up a dragon stew for the local villagers. Fortunately—from the dragon's point of view—such threats are easily, if messily, disposed of.

Fire dragons are so called because they breathe fire, which can roast a fleeing hobbit from twenty-five feet away. The fire is accompanied by noxious sulfur-laden fumes, nearly as deadly as the flames themselves. Fire dragons carry themselves on vast bat-like wings and can sail silently through the air to attack their prey. Their rear legs are short and stumpy, their forearms are slender, and their claws are long, sharp, and deadly when they slash. Mostly fire dragons use their claws to snatch up adventurers and tear them to pieces. However, the claws are also helpful in fine-motor manipulation of the items of the hoard.

Battling a Fire Dragon

Fire dragons traditionally sleep on top of their hoards, coating their stomachs with bits and pieces of their treasure. The observant warrior may notice a hole or two in the dragon's belly, through which he can direct an arrow. Of course one arrow isn't going to bring down a beast such as this unless it's imbued with magical powers. Your best bet is to let a wizard construct such an arrow and be *very careful* about when and where you shoot it. And whatever you do, don't miss. Dragons don't like being shot at; who would? And they're apt to take steps to prevent that sort of thing happening more than once.

Ice Dragons

As the name implies, these dragons live in remote arctic regions, where they prey on bear, bird, seal, and sometimes venture into civilized regions to pick up a snack of villagers or dwarves on their way to a distant mine. They carve their caves into the sides of mountains or icebergs where they store their treasure, letting it freeze into a mass that's practically impossible to move, let alone steal.

Generally, ice dragons have white or blue scales and long, slender wings. They are smaller than fire drakes, stretching about seventy-five feet at most. Their smaller size makes them faster and deadlier in attack. They can disguise themselves by clinging to the sides of icebergs until they drift near a ship or an isolated town.

Ice dragons' breath is cold and can freeze water at up to fifty paces. One method of attack is to freeze ships within a mass of ice floes and then attack the helpless mariners.

Battling an Ice Dragon

If you must, the best way to fight an ice dragon is with fire. Ice dragons don't like anything warm, since it tends to conflict with their natural habitat. If, therefore, you're attacked by an ice dragon, step one is to kindle as large a bonfire as you can put together on short notice. Range yourself around it, backs to the fire, and wait for the attack. Beware the tendency of ice dragons to breath on the fire itself, putting it out and freezing the fuel. If that happens, there's very little more you can do except run. Arrows and swords are little use against the icy scales of this wyrm, and iron is apt to shatter if it's suddenly frozen. *Mithril* mail, if you have any, is the best protection against attack.

Sea Dragons

Sea dragons are what give rise to the legend of sea serpents, and it's not hard to see why. As the name implies, they live in water, although, being reptiles, they must surface regularly to breathe. They are long and slender, with flippers rather than wings, which they use to propel themselves through the sea at enormous speeds. Their favorite prey is ships, which they enjoy playing with, striking them from underneath to knock passengers on deck into the water. These can then be gobbled at leisure. The ship will gradually be broken by repeated blows, its crew eaten, and its treasure collected.

Sea dragons have been seen up to 150 feet in length, but it's difficult to estimate their true size, since so much of them is underwater.

That and the fact that not many survive encounters with these beasts. The breath of a sea dragon has no special offensive power, although it usually smells unpleasantly like fish and seaweed.

Sea dragons make their lairs on isolated islands with good access to shipping lanes. They will eat fish if humans, elves, and dwarves aren't available (they don't eat hobbit, mainly because it's almost impossible to coax a hobbit on board a ship).

Battling a Sea Dragon

The best defense against a sea dragon is a swift boat, and even that's not much help. Sea dragons are notoriously fast swimmers and can overtake any sailing vessel. The one opportunity to counter the attack of a sea dragon may occur if the dragon surfaces and confronts the ship directly, sticking its long, serpentlike neck over the side to snatch at anyone on board. In this case, a well-placed blow with a stout sword can injure and even possibly behead the dragon. Note: Strike to kill. If you only wound a sea dragon (or any other kind of dragon, for that matter), you've annoyed it to the point that it'll make sure nothing is left of you but a grease spot on a shattered deck plank.

Magical Creatures

Up to this point we've been discussing creatures of (more or less) flesh and blood. However, with wights and Ringwraiths we encounter creatures that are even harder to defend against because they're already dead. Or, at least, mostly dead.

Wights

A wight is an undead spirit, usually of someone or something evil. Wights inhabit barrows on the rolling downs just east of the Shire, but they can be found in many other parts of Middle-earth. Wights seek to trap and destroy the souls of living folk, taking them prisoner and binding them with spells.

Wights, as you may gather from this, are magical creatures. They can control fog and other weather-related events in some areas, using them to confuse and trap unwary travelers. They are familiar with binding magic, and many of the objects that were associated with them in life are hoarded by them in death.

Avoiding Wights

When a helpful guide tells you to stay away from a particular area because it's inhabited by wights, do yourself a favor and take his advice. However, if you must wander the haunted barrows, keep a careful eye out for signs of fog or unnatural darkness. In the event of such phenomena, get away from the barrows as quickly as possible and seek sunlight. Like most creatures of darkness, wights dislike sunlight and won't follow you there.

In the Clutches of a Wight

When you're trapped in a wight's tomb, *do not panic*. I mean, you may think that your life is going to come to a swift and nasty end, but panicking isn't going to help matters. The main thing is to keep your head and remember the following:

- **CALL FOR HELP.** This is a really, really good time to remember any spells, rhymes, or poems that are going to produce magical help. The wight is a creature that's probably beyond your abilities, so don't try to fight it on your own. This is not time for egotism.
- **WIGHTS DON'T LIKE THE SUNLIGHT.** If possible, smash a door or break a window or do *something* to get natural light into the tomb. Wights vanish in the sunlight, or so we've been told.
- **WIGHTS TEND TO ACCUMULATE MAGICAL WEAPONS WITHOUT MUCH ATTENTION TO WHOM THEY GET THEM FROM OR WHAT THEIR HISTORIES ARE.** So if you find a sword in a wight's tomb, feel free to use it. Chances are, it's going to be useful.

- **DON'T ABANDON YOUR FRIENDS.** That's not going to help you, especially when it comes to karma. Instead it's best to rally round your friends and defend them against threats. You may die doing this, but the fates will look favorably upon you.
- **WHEN FREED FROM A WIGHT'S TOMB, RUN AWAY.** And stay away.

Ringwraiths

These are about the nastiest creatures you're likely to ever encounter, even surpassing dragons. There are only nine of them, but they're just about impossible to kill, and they have magical powers that surpass just about everything you can find on Middle-earth, including most wizards. Therefore, the best advice regarding them is to get away fast.

Some general advice about them includes:

- **WHATEVER YOU DO, DON'T PUT ON MAGICAL RINGS.** Are you crazy? That's about the worst thing you can do, since it sucks you into their world and makes you more vulnerable to attack. You'd have to be nuts to do that. Wait! What are you doing? Stop it!!
- **RINGWRAITHS ARE CREATURES OF THE DARK LORD, AND THEIR STRENGTH WAXES AND WANES WITH HIS.** You might think that the lesson here is to attack the Dark Lord if you want to weaken Ringwraiths, but that's not really it. The Dark Lord is beyond just about anyone's strength, and in truth, the best thing you can do to deal with Ringwraiths is stay away from them. And don't, if possible, take possession of any magical rings.
- **RINGWRAITHS ARE MOSTLY NOT PART OF THE WORLD IN WHICH WE LIVE, SO NORMAL ATTACKS ON THEM DON'T WORK.** For example, if you hit a Ringwraith with a sword, it'll hurt you a lot more than it'll hurt the wraith. Still, you can do some damage to a wraith with a sword; just don't expect to have a chance for a follow-up attack.

- **GO FOR THEIR HORSES.** The horses that Ringwraiths ride are
  real, and thus they are vulnerable. A well-shot arrow will take
  down a Black Rider, as long as it's aimed at his horse. Other
  attacks on wraith horses can be made with swords, daggers, or
  magically induced floods.

Ringwraith Steeds

Unhorsed during the flood at the Bruinen of Rivendell, the Ringwraiths were remounted on flying steeds, a sort of cross between
dragons and eagles. The beasts were able to attack, to fly swiftly, to
defend themselves against arrows and stones, and were fed on "foul
meats," which generally means carrion. The riders, thus mounted,
were renamed the Nazgul. If attacked by a Nazgul, there's little you
can do other than to seek shelter in the swiftest way. Nazgul can be
killed, but probably not by you. It's best to leave this to other heroes,
preferably to women, disguised as men, who are going to confuse the
hell out of the Nazgul and confound the terms of prophecies. So stick
with that.

Nonmagical Animals

Animals can be put to the service of the Dark Lord, and he controls
many of them. Some, such as crows, he uses as spies, sending them
in flights to sweep back and forth across the approaches to his land.
Others, such as wolves, are useful for attacking strangers or any
adventurers who come too close. Finally there are battle beasts, such
as oliphaunts, who can be used as tanks during an army's onslaught.

Fighting an oliphaunt isn't easy, since in the words of the rhyme it's
as "big as a house." Massed arrow fire won't do much good unless the
arrows are directed at the oliphaunt's eyes. This will madden the beast,
and it can be worn down, pulled to earth, and dispatched with axes.

Oliphaunt tusks make lovely wedding gifts.

The Dark Lord

If you encounter Sauron himself, you've bumped square up against one of the Powers of Middle-earth, and you should stay away—far away. Of course, you won't have any choice. In the time it would take for you to read this, you'll be smack in the middle of the Dark Tower, and anything you want will be irrelevant. The only hope you have is to go mad before torture drags out your darkest secrets.

If—*if*—you happen to have a magic ring, and if you happen to drop it in the Cracks of Doom in Mount Doom, Orodruin, the Fire Mountain, you've got a chance. Otherwise, this is probably a good time to say good-bye.

Survival

in the

Wild

SHOES

here are no safe paths in this part of the world. Remember you are over the Edge of the Wild now, and in for all sorts of fun wherever you go."

—Gandalf in JRR Tolkien's *The Hobbit*

If, like Bilbo, you're a sheltered, refined, easygoing hobbit (or, at any rate, are someone who's never ventured much farther than your front gate), you'll be completely unprepared when fate thrusts you into an Unexpected Journey. After years of sleeping comfortably in a bed, having four or five square meals a day—plus tea, "afters," and late-night snacks—and strolling down to the Green Dragon to knock back a few pints and smoke a pipe of Longbottom Leaf, suddenly you're sleeping on the hard ground, dining on fruits, nuts, and possibly chunks of venison that have been roasted over an open fire, and you can't remember the last time you had a drink, a smoke, or an uninterrupted night's sleep. In your old comfortable, contented life, the most exciting thing that ever happened was the miller getting caught mixing whole bran in the white bread. In your new, adventurous life, you're coming face-to-face with wolves, orcs, goblins, dragons, spiders, and often much worse. You didn't know that there was anything worse.

Just in case you find yourself in such a situation, here are some tips, drawn from Bilbo and Frodo's experiences. If your adventures take you farther afield and into stranger places than they ventured, well, you're on your own.

Food

Let's start with the basics. If you find yourself adrift in the Wild—and for most of us, that means someplace we can't plug in a hair drier—you need to consider the essentials: food and shelter. Food's the most immediate. You can't go more than forty-eight hours without nutritional relief. But don't imagine for a minute you're going to be able to sit down in a tavern and order a steak-and-kidney pie (or whatever dish you like). This is the Wild. There are no steak-and-kidney pies to be had. For that matter, there aren't very many inns—at least not ones you'd care to enter without a drawn sword.

Packing Food

Packing food for a long journey is difficult, of course, because there's no refrigeration where you're going. At best, if you camp next to a stream, you can put some of the food in it to keep it cold (but then you risk it getting waterlogged). For this reason, the experienced adventurer prefers meat in the form of jerky, which can be prepared over the kitchen fire on those long, cold winter evenings. In addition, bring along plenty of nuts (a valuable source of protein), cheese (if it's preserved in its rind), bread (good only until it molds), and fruit.

Scavenging for Sustenance in the Wilderness

It certainly helps to be able to recognize basic foodstuffs. These include (but aren't limited to) the following:

- Herbs
- Wild onions
- Strawberries (or any sort of fruit)
- Mushrooms (Caution: Some mushrooms are poisonous. If you don't know Basic Mushroom Recognition, play it safe and stay away. Getting some food in your belly isn't going to do you much good if it makes you sick as a dog for three days.)
- Rabbit

- Pheasant (Unless you're good with a bow and arrow, you're probably not going to catch one of these, but keep in mind that it's an option.)
- Fish (These can be caught by hand, although it helps if you're bone-thin with slimy, gray skin, lank hair, two or three teeth, and have been living under the mountains for several centuries.)

Foods to be Avoided

Not everything you find in the Wild is good to eat. The particularly hungry adventurer may find himself tempted to try just about anything to sate a raging hunger. Resist this impulse. Among the things to avoid:

- Poisonous mushrooms (see previous page)
- Black squirrels
- Wild boar (unless you're trained in hunting boar and have a boar spear; the exception to this rule is if you're a dwarf—or in the company of one—who's adept with an axe and can hew the head off a charging boar without bothering to blow his own beard hairs out of his mouth)
- Wolf
- Rabid wolf

What to Do With Food, Once You've Got It

Some foods can be eaten raw (e.g., fruit, mushrooms). Other foods are best either eaten with something else (e.g., herbs, mushrooms) or must be cooked (e.g., venison, rabbit, fish). To cook foods with best results:

1. Use dry wood rather than green. Green wood will smoke, giving away your position to any unfriendly eyes that may be looking for you.
2. Have some water handy to put out the fire quickly if need be. You never know what danger may come upon you suddenly.

3. Surround the fire with stones, if possible, to prevent it from spreading. Another alternative is to dig a shallow pit and build the fire in that.

4. Keep the fire small. No reason to create a massive blaze just to cook a couple of rabbits.

5. Use two forked sticks, one on either side of the fire, and a long, pointed stick laid across them to create a basic spit. With this mechanism, you can roast rabbit, goose, or just about any other small game, turning the stick to keep the meat from burning.

6. Alternatively, if by some chance you have a pan, cut up the meat, add water (or, if possible, a little grease), and sauté the meat until partially cooked through. Add water, salt (if you have it), and herbs to make a savory stew.

7. If neither of these alternatives appeals and members of your adventuring party want to have a more do-it-yourself approach to cooking, sharpen some long sticks and invite them to barbecue their own piece of meat to taste. For extra flavor, they can stick a mushroom on either side of the meat, or possibly (if the meat is sweet, such as pork from a wild boar), a piece of fruit such as an apple.

Hunting Food in the Wild

Plenty of food is on the hoof in the lands beyond which ordinary people stray. If any in your party have reasonable skill with a bow, they can probably bring down a pheasant, goose, or even a deer, rabbit, or wild boar. (See page 97.) However, there are certain instances where game should be left alone. For instance, if you're going into a dark wood on a winding, difficult path, and your host, who lives near the edge of the wood and probably knows as much about it as anyone alive, tells you not to shoot anything in the wood because it won't taste good and you'll waste your arrows—don't shoot at game in the wood. Just stick to the food you brought with you.

Hunting Magical Creatures

Hunting magical creatures for food (or pretty much any other reason) is strongly discouraged. For one thing, they probably won't taste good, and for another, killing them usually brings bad luck. Dragons are, of course, the exception to this rule. Following is a recipe for dragon.

SAVORY GARLIC DRAGON

Ingredients:

    1 medium-size dragon

    2 tons table salt

    ½ ton black pepper

    2 wagonloads garlic

    4 hogsheads white wine

    4 bay leaves

Dig a fire pit approximately 100 feet by 50 feet. Fill with branches, fire, and let burn until reduced to glowing coals. Cut dragon into small, bite-size pieces, reserving bones for stock and the skull for display. In large (15-foot) skillets (as many as necessary), sauté garlic. Add dragon, seasoning frequently with salt and pepper. When cooked to pinkness, remove from flame and set aside. Deglaze pans with wine. Add bay leaves. Reduce sauce until it coats the back of a wooden spoon. Serve dragon on platters, with sauce poured over. For an extra flourish, garnish with parsley.

Hunting Deer

While it's fine to hunt deer, and venison is a good source of nutrition for adventurers, you are strongly advised to avoid hunting any of the following:

- White deer that appear, as if by magic, at the edge of a clearing

- Deer that lead you on a long chase through strange woods, across wide valleys, and to a path that ends at the gates of a mysterious castle. Shooting the deer under these circumstances can, at best, turn out to be unfortunate. There is also a small chance that the deer may actually be the daughter of the castle's owner, a girl who's been enchanted and is trying to lead you back to her father so you can break the enchantment and marry her. Shooting her under these conditions is unlikely to lead to wedding bells.

- Deer that flit past in the twilight, making barely a sound, and vanish before you can leap to your feet and pursue them. Just let them go. They're nothing but trouble. Something better will come along.

Stealing Food

Many adventurers consider normal rules of morality suspended in their case. After all, when you're fighting bad guys (or creatures), you can't be too picky about your methods. So it's a time-honored tradition among adventurers to steal food when it's handy. For example, suppose you come across a group of trolls. The trolls are sitting quietly by the fire, not bothering anyone, bantering among themselves, perfectly content to wait until it's time for them to go back to their troll hole. Meanwhile they're dining on delicious roast mutton and mugs of beer. What do you do?

An experienced adventurer might drug the beer, wait for the trolls to pass out, steal the mutton, and for good measure, steal any gold or silver that the tolls had acquired and stored in their hole. The adventurer might also slip a dagger into each of the trolls, thereby elevating vulgar assassination to the level of epic story.

Stealing food doesn't, of course, have to mean slaughtering those who have prepared it. But in the course of your travels you come across a savory apple pie sitting unattended on a windowsill of a passing farmhouse, remember: The ends justify the means.

Drink

Along with whatever food you've scrounged, hunted, or stolen you'll naturally want something to drink. Broadly speaking, drinks come in three varieties: ale, wine, and water. In general, elves prefer wine, dwarves prefer ale, men like wine and ale, and hobbits like anything, as long as there are generous quantities of it. Pretty much no one prefers water, but they'll drink it at a pinch. (Orcs and goblins generally drink foul-smelling, disgusting stuff but they also drink water; dragons drink entire lakes dry; and giant spiders, of course, drink blood.)

Ale, Ale, the Gang's All Here!

Some races are better at brewing ale than others. That's all there is to it. You may hear stories of the hobbit 1420 (one of the best brews in the history of the Shire) or of Old Moria Stout and Iron Hills Pale Ale. But you never hear about Rivendell Rogue Ale or Lothlórien Lager. There's a good reason for that; elves think beer is vulgar. They don't drink it, they don't make it, and they hold dwarves in some contempt for introducing malt beverages to the world. Hobbits, too, have gotten very good at brewing beer, and every tavern in the Shire and the surrounding area functions as a kind of mini-brewpub.

Find the Best Beers

Finding good beer is like finding anything else: You have to be willing to spend a while looking. And, fortunately, that means a lot of tasting. In fact, it's entirely possible that the whole purpose of your adventure is to expand your palate and discover new and better beers. For the uninitiated:

- Pale ale uses primarily pale malt and is a pale yellow in color.
- Stout is made with roasted malts and is a dark, heavy, thick beer. It's ideal for an adventurer; a little bit goes a long way, and it has considerable nutritional value. Or at least the people who drink it a lot think it does.

- Wheat beer, as the name implies, is made with wheat and malted barley. It's a lighter beer with a distinctive taste.
- Lager is one of the most widely known and drunk beers. Most pubs you come across during your travels will have its own lager, which the owner will be anxious for you to sample. Take him up on his offer.

Wine

The best wines in Middle-earth are those of Dorwinion, but there are plenty of others to go around. Although only elves have access to the rambling cellars of the Last Homely House, we can suppose that Elrond keeps an extensive wine cellar on which he draws for banquets and special occasions, as well as for his own personal taste. There is plenty of wine to go around the banqueting halls of Gondor as well, where the king sits on his golden throne, drinking from a jeweled cup. You might not ascend to those heights, but there's no reason even in the Wild not to enjoy a decent draught of good wine.

The Mead-halls of Rohan

The Riders of Rohan may sample wine when they ally with their cousins to the south in Minas Tirith. But at home in Edoras, they prefer mead, a drink made from fermented honey. The main advantages of mead are that it's easy to brew, it stores well, and it gets you good and drunk, and in the mood for a wild cavalry charge in the face of hopeless odds.

Carrying Drink With You

The accepted way to bring drink along on any adventure is in a wineskin. The wise adventurer not only takes several of these in his or her pack but replenishes them at every opportunity. Even if this means sneaking down to the cellars of the Elven-king in his palace in Mirkwood, it's well worth it—and easier to accomplish if you happen to be invisible.

It's not a good idea to take drink in bottles or jugs, and barrels are unwieldy, although once you've drunk all the beer or wine you can ride the barrels along a river. That is, if you don't mind bobbing around and getting soaking wet.

Double-check your skins for leaks; you don't want to run out of alcohol at a crucial moment—say, right before beginning a battle with a giant or a confrontation with a hoard of hobgoblins.

Water

As mentioned previously, water is the preferred drink of almost no one. That said, it's the easiest one to find in the Wild. A couple of significant points about finding water:

- **FRESH WATER COMES FROM STREAMS AND/OR RIVERS.** *Don't* drink water from an ocean.
- **IF YOU HAVEN'T HAD WATER IN A WHILE AND YOU COME ACROSS A DISGUSTING, OILY, FOUL-SMELLING STREAM, DON'T BE PICKY.** Water's water, and you don't know when you're going to find some more. Drink your fill and fill your skins.
- **IF, HOWEVER, IN SUCH AN INSTANCE, YOU HAVE A FRIEND OR COMPANION WHO OFFERS TO DRINK FIRST, LET THEM.** If they fall over in convulsions after drinking, you'll know it's time to search for a different water source.
- **IF YOU'VE BEEN SPECIFICALLY WARNED NOT TO DRINK FROM A STREAM IN THE MIDDLE OF A FOREST BECAUSE IT CAUSES SLEEP AND FORGETFULNESS, DON'T DO IT.** Don't question why, don't argue, just . . . don't.
- **BE HELPFUL TO OTHER ADVENTURERS.** Consider posting a sign by such a stream with large letters reading SERIOUSLY POISONOUS STREAM; MAY CAUSE FORGETFULNESS AND SLEEP AND OTHER BAD STUFF; OH, ALL RIGHT, DRINK IF YOU WANT, BUT DON'T SAY WE DIDN'T WARN YOU.

Shelter

Contrary to what you may have heard, four walls don't make a house. Especially not if this house has no roof or the roof leaks in a rainstorm. After you've satisfied the cravings of your stomach, you'll need a place to stay that's:

1. Dry
2. Warm (or at least not freezing cold)
3. Safe (relatively)

You may assume that when in the Wild, it's a case of any port in a storm, but in fact you should be careful when choosing your shelter. Here are some things to look out for.

Caves

Caves are great to shelter in because they're (a) dry; (b) warm, if you build a fire near the entrance; and (c) pretty easy to defend against a frontal assault. However, they have significant disadvantages. The biggest one is, as Gandalf well understands, you never know how far back they go. Bilbo and his dwarf companions got a rather nasty shock when the cave they were sleeping in, high up in the Misty Mountains, turned out to be the front porch of a highly irritable band of goblins. So, even if you find a nice dry cave and it doesn't seem big enough to hide anything unpleasant and unexpected, remember that there are always hidden doors, cracks, and pits from which creepy things can crawl out of the darkness.

Bigger Caves

The bigger the cave, the greater the possibility that there's something in it that doesn't want you there. Alternatively, there's something in it that's very happy to have you there, because it's feeling peckish and you look like a particularly appetizing hors d'oeuvre. The first order of business when choosing a cave for the evening is to thoroughly explore it. That means eyeing all the little cracks and crev-

ices, inspecting the walls for possible secret entrances, and keeping in mind that just because you can't climb down and explore a hole in the floor doesn't mean someone or something can't climb up.

Really, Really Big Caves—We're Talking the Kind You Could Fit a City Into

Really big caves can be great; they have incredibly beautiful stalagmites and stalactites, huge caverns with glittering walls and translucent ceilings, and miles and miles of twisting corridors that plunge on and on through the bowels of the earth. And that's really the problem. A big cave offers plenty of shelter—you could probably hide a whole army and a half in the Mines of Moria—but its sheer size means it's impossible to explore thoroughly. Just as Gandalf, Frodo, Aragorn, and company found a balrog living in Moria, so you may encounter quite a bit more than you've bargained for, if you go into one of these places. The best thing to do if you venture into one is to bring along plenty of friends, torches, weapons, and at all times a clear idea in your mind of the shortest route to the nearest exit.

And if you start hearing drums in the deep, run like hell.

Haunted Caves

Caves are apt to be haunted by spirits of the dead, or undead, or not-quite-dead-but-getting-there. After all, caves are dark and creepy, and lots of horrible things have happened in them, so there are lots of good reasons for the dead to hang around in caves. If, by chance, you find yourself in a cave haunted by the spirits of the dead, keep a cool head about you. Panicking isn't going to help. It's a natural reaction, to be sure, but running in a random direction screaming at the top of your lungs is just going to piss off the spirits and whatever friends they have. The best thing is to be confident, assertive, polite, and to have a good explanation for your presence. Something along the following lines should suffice: "Oh, is this your cave? I'm so sorry. We're just passing through, and we were under the impression that it was uninhabited. We certainly didn't mean to trespass, and we'll be moving along now. Oh, by the way, you look really great. Death suits you."

Who Lives in Caves

Naturally you may want an idea of who lives in caves and who you're most likely to run into (in addition to spirits of the dead). Common inhabitants may include:

- **GOBLINS.** Goblins have a natural affinity with the underground; most of their cities are underground, and they like tunnels and machinery and explosions and things like that. This isn't to say they're all that good at creating underground habitations; goblin tunnels are mostly twisty, confusing, rough, damp, and filled with sharp stones and low-hanging roofs. Goblins are easily scared but persistent. If you find yourself in their caves, remember that they know the lay of the land much better than you do. Keep an eye peeled for the exit.

- **SPIDERS.** Some spiders, it's true, prefer trees, but big, nasty spiders enjoy the underground life, with its steady diet of bugs, hibernating bears, goblins, and the occasional adventurer. Spiders can squeeze their bodies into very small spaces and block tunnels with their webs, so their tunnels are extremely difficult to navigate. Spiders don't, of course, create caves themselves, but they're happy to take over ones made by goblins, dwarves, and others.

- **DWARVES.** Dwarves are a friendly race for the most part (unless you're an elf, in which case relations are a bit dicey). They're superb builders and tunnelers, with a natural skill at creating huge underground cities—for instance, the vast city and realm of the Dwarrowdelf that adjoined the Mines of Moria. Stumbling into a group of dwarf miners can be a lucky accident for an adventurer, who'll find herself plied with offers of beer, food, and often gold and jewels, which the dwarves have in abundance. Dwarves look upon themselves as farmers, in a sense, cultivating a vast underground crop that must slowly be tended and cared for so that it can be opened to even greater vistas. All in all, if you're wandering around underground, lost, hungry, and cold, dwarves are good fellows to meet.

- **CRAWLY THINGS.** All sorts of creatures burrow into caves, away from the light and fresh air. Some are pretty harmless, although it's best not to disturb them. Others brood in the darkness, hating anything and anyone who comes from the world of light. There's no way to anticipate meeting one of these creatures, but if you do, it's a good idea to have a supply of riddles (or some other game) at the ready, as well as a sharp sword.

Trees

Just as caves are often associated with dwarves, so trees have an affinity with elves. Trees offer shelter to the weary traveler and serve as a canopy against storms, a place of safety that can be climbed and can be defended against enemies, and a source of firewood and, possibly, food. That said, there are ups and downs to choosing trees for shelter in the Wild.

Choosing the Right Tree

Trees are unpredictable. Some are happy to provide shelter, with their huge boles and tangled roots offering snug hiding places and nooks in which the adventurer can curl up and rest his weary head. Others are treacherous and evil, tempting travelers to lean against them for a nap before snaring them into cracks in their bark, slowly devouring them and drawing them in. Still others are simply wild, and they need a strong hand guiding them and preventing them from doing harm, accidental or intentional, to the passing traveler. When choosing a tree for shelter, stop and consider what sort of tree it is and whether it has reason to dislike you.

Trees, it must be said, have ample reason to be suspicious of humans, since we routinely chop them down, cut them up for fires or for furniture, or carve our initials into them. But it's possible by laying aside things such as axes and flint and tinder to convince the trees that our goal isn't to destroy them. Unlike caves, trees are living things that can even be conversed with, on occasion.

Climbing Trees

You must climb a tree to get to the best shelter it has to offer. Choose a broad branch, well away from the wind and rain, and settle down. In the event that orcs or goblins come ranging around the base of the tree, you'll probably hear them. If wargs start howling, you'll certainly hear them. And if goblins try to burn down the forest, you'll smell the smoke.

Tops of trees are generally best, since you can easily be rescued by eagles if things get tense. It's true that no one likes to be in the top of a fir tree in the midst of a raging forest fire, but the top is safer than the lower branches, where wild wolves can snap at you and the spears of goblins might reach your legs. Even in the middle of all this, remember that trees have feelings, and you're probably going to make some friends by being careful about where you put your hands and feet.

Fire and Trees

If you find yourself in the middle of a large, strange forest, and you have the urge to start a campfire, keep in mind that the best wood is dead wood. Don't start chopping down trees, whatever you do. Remember that a tree's natural enemy is fire. On the other hand, in colder weather, trees sort of like fire. Just be cautious when you light one.

Tree Dwellings

The experts on tree houses are unquestionably elves. The elves of Lothlórien live exclusively in trees, on wide *flets* or platforms that are mounted by means of ladders or flights of stairs. These are the best sorts of refuges to be found in trees. If you can't live in Lothlórien, try to build some small platforms on the trees you're in. You'll lessen the chances of rolling off a branch during the night.

Moving Trees

It's possible that you may wind up in some of the trees that move (huorns). Don't be alarmed; rather, try to offer them some reasonable advice: Turn left at Isengard and keep going until you reach Mordor. Oh, and destroy any orcs and random evil wizards you encounter on your way. And if you see any Ents, do what they tell you. Ents know what they're talking about most of the time.

Talking to Trees

Trees don't as a rule have much to say. If a tree does talk to you, be cautious. It may be trying to seduce you with the intention of absorbing you via its bark cracks. Also be sure to distinguish between trees and Ents. Trees are trees. Ents are simply treelike—tall, bushy, strong, slow moving, and slow talking. Given their size and strength, it's important to be polite to them. Who knows? An Ent may invite you back to its hall for some refreshing Ent-draught. Better than beer, with twice the nutrients.

Other Shelters

In addition to caves and trees (and houses, if they're available), the enterprising adventurer might seek out of the following.

Cliffs

A cliff with a slight overhang can make a shelter from a raging blizzard or rainstorm, although not much of one. The chief dangers in a blizzard are snowdrifts that make forward or backward progress difficult or impossible. Rainstorms, of course, will leave you drenched and freezing, and although a cliff wall may shield you from the worst of the wind and occasional falling boulders, you probably won't be able to start a fire. Still, a cliff wall is better than nothing. If you happen to have ponies or horses, set them in front of you to block the wind and give you a little more warmth.

Eagle Eyries

Do *not* under any circumstances climb up to an eagle's nest uninvited. Particularly if you're small and the eagle or its chicks are hungry. If so, you will probably end up torn apart for a late breakfast. On the other hand, if the eagle itself brings you to the eyrie, you can be assured of reasonable safety (provided you don't fall off) and a spectacular view.

Ruins

Numerous ruins lay scattered around the world, and they can offer some shelter to the weary traveler. You may even find the remains of buildings, with something resembling a roof to give cover. However, take caution. Ruins are usually in ruins for good reason, and you may not be the first to take up shelter there. Among other things, watch out for:

- Wights
- Trolls
- Orcs
- Ringwraiths (uncommon but still possible)

What the Well-Dressed Adventurer Is Wearing These Days

There's no *Adventurer's GQ*, but there should be. Here are some helpful hints about what you should wear to your first adventure.

Hood and Cloak

This is basic survival gear. The cloak will keep you warm, disguised, and, if of elvish make, will protect you from unfriendly eyes. The hood will keep the rain out of your eyes, and the whole ensemble can fit into your pack. No one has invented any better garment for surviving in the Wild.

Armor

Several different kinds of armor, all of them providing various degrees of protection, can be had:

- **LEATHER ARMOR.** This is the most flexible, easy to wear, cheapest, and most vulnerable to arrows and sword blows. Still, the beginning adventurer could do worse.
- **PARTIAL PLATE.** This includes a breast plate (to stop sword swings), shin or arm guards, and a helmet, which will discourage random strokes to the head.
- **FULL PLATE.** This is serious stuff, but it's also uncomfortable to wear, heavy, and has a tendency to rust and become incredibly hot in full sun. Still, there's nothing better for stopping a full-on sword or lance attack. Just be sure you've got an armorer handy to fix any problems, and a group of helpful friends to lift you onto your horse when you've been unseated.

Who You'll Encounter in the Wild

The Wild is filled with lots of strange creatures, most of whom haven't met you and wouldn't care to, even if you had a letter of introduction from the Wizard Radagast (who seems to have been at home with much of the Wild). In most circumstances, the creatures of the Wild will simply pass you by. In a few cases, they'll want to confront you and talk to you. And in a few other cases, they'll want to eat you. Most of the time, the best course is to go your way with as little muss and fuss as possible. Hobbits in particular are good at this sort of thing; passing through the countryside they're liable to raise the attention of a nearby fox but not much more. But if you should happen to excite the general comment of the countryside, here's how to handle it.

Men

Men tend to keep to themselves and to congregate in their own communities. Except for a few places, such as Bree on the outskirts of civilization, they don't have much to do with the Wild, and they'd prefer to keep it that way, thank you very much. The memories of men stretch only to a few generations, so they don't recall the long history that may be left in the Wild to fester over many centuries. If you run into men in the Wild, they're likely to be Rangers, men of the vanished race of the Númenóreans. Give them the respect they deserve and pass along with little comment. It's possible that they may take you prisoner for a while, but rest assured that their motives are honorable.

Rangers

Rangers are a special variety of men, the remnants of the Númenóreans (see above). They're sworn to protect people from danger, so if you happen to encounter them, you're in luck. However, don't expect them to be a barrel of laughs. Guarding against unknown foes is tough work, and Rangers are apt to grouse about how little thanks they get and how hard they live. Despite this, don't offer them any money; they'll take it as an insult and will be even snottier to you than is their wont.

Elves

What few elves you bump into in the Wild are on their way to the Havens and would prefer to be left alone to continue their journey in peace. They are wrapped in a melancholy of their own making, and there's very little you or anyone else can say that's going to make them feel any better. You can take some comfort in the fact that they're at least as disinterested in you as you may be in them. Just smile, hail them, and pass by. Nothing to see here. Nothing at all.

Dwarves

Most dwarves these days are busy in the various mines they've staked out: the Blue Hills, the Iron Hills, the Lonely Mountain. Even the Mines of Moria are showing some signs of regeneration. Be that as it may, dwarves are businesslike and brisk, ready enough to trade goods for gold and silver (dwarves are the original mercantilists) but not much interested in anything that doesn't directly affect their interests. They have respect for men and hobbits, though little for elves, and they feel that the best approach to any orcs they meet on the road is a swift blow from an axe.

Orcs

Most of the orcs of Middle-earth were destroyed either in the Battle of Five Armies or later in the fall of the Dark Tower. A few are clinging to existence in the dark corners of the land, and you may encounter them on a lonely road or in the depths of the night. The downfall of the Tower of Saruman meant that Saruman's followers were scattered over the land, and while some of them wound up in the Shire for a few months, they were driven out after the Battle of Bywater and are now merely robbers and footpads who are likely to be mopped up by the King's men. That said, in the Wild it's as well to keep a close watch after nightfall and to travel the roads in companies of fifteen or twenty, well armed with swords in case of trouble.

Wolves

The wargs, the worst of the wild wolves, largely ceased to be a nuisance after the collapse of Sauron's realm. The traveler today who worries about attacks of wolves is probably a bit on the paranoid side. Still, there's no reason to take chances. A few lone wolves still roam the forests, attacking individual adventurers, and striking fear into the hearts of foresters. Keep a guard out for them, and remember that there's nothing so effective against wolves as setting treetops on fire.

Weird Nature Spirits

Wandering the fringes of the world, you'll encounter from time to time unclassifiable creatures, some friendly, others unfriendly or, at best, neutral. Tom Bombadil and Goldberry can be numbered among these weird nature spirits; Beorn of the Carrock near Mirkwood is another. They can be exuberant and a bit overwhelming (Tom); mystic, mysterious, and stunningly beautiful (Goldberry); or suspicious and grouchy but with a good heart (Beorn). Survival in the Wild may depend on your ability to successfully interact with these spirits, so avoid offending them and take what assistance they proffer. Remember that they answer to no one, so you can't appeal to their sense of responsibility. Ents belong, in some degree, to this category, and as Treebeard remarks, "I am not wholly on anyone's side, because no one is on my side." However, you can generally expect them, when push comes to shove, to come down on the side of good against evil, even if they make you pay a price for their assistance.

The rules for dealing with these creatures include:

- **DON'T OVERWHELM THEM WITH NUMBERS.** They live by themselves and are nervous in society. If you're traveling with a large party (say, thirteen dwarves, one hobbit, and one wizard), introduce yourselves a bit at a time.
- **DON'T BE HASTY.** Things take time. Relax. Chill. Middle-earth will wait for a day or two.
- **DON'T HESITATE TO CALL ON THEM—ASSUMING YOU'RE STILL IN THEIR PART OF THE WILD—FOR HELP IF YOU NEED IT.** Note: Getting stuck in a barrow haunted by an evil wight definitely counts as "needing help."
- **BE POLITE AND DON'T ASK QUESTIONS THAT DON'T NEED ANSWERING.** Asking Beorn about shape-shifting is rude and none of your concern; if a huge bear comes prowling around the house at night, ignore it and go back to sleep. If he wanted to kill you, he'd have done it already.

Outposts of Civilization

In the far-flung corners of the land, it's possible to find a few centers of society that still maintain some decency and the hope of feather-beds. In particular, a few inns exist on the very fringes of the Wild, as well as some small outposts of civilization such as the Last Homely House. The traveler may wish to stop at these to renew his or her stocks of food, wine, and water, and to hear the latest news about the road ahead.

The Prancing Pony

From time immemorial, the Butterbur family has owned the Prancing Pony at Bree. Since this community caters to both Big People and hobbits, the Pony has rooms for both. The hobbit rooms are generally on the first floor and have round windows. The inn itself is the social center of the town of Bree, one of the last towns on the Great Road before it passes into the Wild. The common room of the inn is a vortex of gossip and news from the Shire to the west to the towns of Archet and Combs to the east. If there's any information you want to hear, your best bet is to buy a pint of beer in the Pony common room and sip it very slowly.

When Frodo and his companions arrive at the Prancing Pony, they find a motley crew of Bree townsfolk, dwarves, and yes, even hobbits.

> The company was in the big common-room of the inn. The gathering was large and mixed, as Frodo discovered, when his eyes got used to the light. This came chiefly from a blazing log-fire, for the three lamps hanging from the beams were dim, and half veiled in smoke. Barliman Butterbur was standing near the fire, talking to a couple of dwarves and one or two strange-looking men. On the benches were various folk: men of Bree, a collection of local hobbits (sitting chattering together), a few more dwarves, and other vague figures difficult to make out away in the shadows and corners. (*The Fellowship of the Ring*, chapter 9)

The Last Inn

Far out on the Road that leads from the west across the Anduin and to the bleak lands of the northeast, the Last Inn is the final stop for many travelers. The beer here is no more than acceptable and the food matches it in mediocrity, but as the out-flung arm of civilization, it's still a welcome sight—being the last place adventurers are likely to sleep in a bed.

Rivendell

The house of Elrond Half-Elven is, as Bilbo long ago remarked, "perfect, whether you liked food, or sleep, or work, or story-telling, or singing, or just sitting and thinking best, or a pleasant mixture of them all." It's filled with elves who are, on the whole, less annoying than they tend to be elsewhere. Elrond, being a loremaster, is always willing to help read a difficult map or translate a bit of obscure text. At the same time, Rivendell is hidden in a valley and fenced about with powerful magic so that it's difficult to find if the elves don't want you to be aware of it. The wise adventurer will send ahead for an invitation, specifying how long he or she will be staying, any special dietary requirements, and what sort of accommodations they would like to reserve. Check-out time is promptly at 11 a.m.

Survival Skills

Without some basic abilities, you won't last long in the Wild. It's not only a matter of staying on your feet and not being caught and cooked or getting drowned in a river somewhere. You must know how to live off the land. In addition to what we've discussed previously, practice the following skills at home before setting off on an adventure.

Fire Building

To make a fire you need the following:

- Kindling
- Some dry moss or leaves; anything that will catch fire and burn swiftly
- Larger branches or logs that will provide long-burning heat
- Flint and steel to strike a spark

Place the moss and/or leaves in a small pile, leaving plenty of room for air to circulate freely. Strike the flint against the steel next to them, until sparks land on the tinder. Blow gently—no matter how frustrated you become—on the tinder until flames appear. Feed the flames with small pieces of kindling, gradually increasing in size until the fire is established. Only then add the larger branches and logs. As mentioned above, keep the area around the fire clear of anything flammable to the distance of at least two feet, including leaves, sticks, moss, clothing, or adventurers. In the Wild there's no need to make a big bonfire. Keep it small and keep it safe.

Note: Another way to make fire is to use magic. This is generally confined to wizards and will broadcast your position to anyone watching, but in extreme circumstances, such as the middle of a snowstorm or a flash flood, you may not have much choice. Choose a large chunk of wood, stick a magic staff into it, and recite the appropriate spell. This generally works.

Woodcraft

To prevent being followed, and to know if anything else has recently passed in the direction you're going, learn to avoid unnecessarily snapping off branches and flattening patches of grass with your feet, to say nothing of leaving footprints in the dust. Watch carefully for twigs that have been bent at unnatural angles or stones that have been kicked out of place in the earth. Practice listening for sounds of pursuing feet—or feet in front of you running away. Cultivate the observation of detail; it could mean the difference between life and death.

Horsemanship

Much of your time in the Wild will probably be spent on foot, since there are too many places that are not traversable by horse or pony. Still, it doesn't hurt to be a skillful rider. Spend time practicing mounting and dismounting; if you can get your steed to trust you, this will become easier. Learn to control your horse not only with the reins but with your legs and with your whole body. Train him or her to respond instinctively to danger and not to throw you off his back while running from wolves or goblins. A skill at quickly turning and stopping will come in handy if you need to throw off pursuing riders. Spend some time learning to shoot a bow and arrow accurately and quickly while riding a horse and looking behind you. You may not be as good as the Riders of Rohan, but there's no reason to make a fool of yourself on horseback either. And these skills are, to some extent, transferable to riding ponies, eagles, and traveling on the shoulders of Ents.

Hunting

We mentioned earlier that hunting in the Wild is an essential source of food. In addition to shooting animals on the fly with bow and arrow or hewing down a charging board with a battle-axe, learn to set snares for rabbits and smaller animals. Set a few traps in the early evening, and by the next morning, you may have a fine brace of quail for breakfast. As well, you'll need to know how to pluck fowls and skin animals, as well as what parts are good eating and what should be thrown away. Remember, waste not, want not. Try to use every part of what you kill. Help keep Middle-earth clean: Avoid littering.

Fishing

If you find yourself near a pond or lake, remember that there's nothing like fresh fish cooked over an open fire moments after you've caught it. You can easily fashion a rod from a sturdy branch (preferably green wood so that it bends instead of breaking). Bait it with a worm, a bit of meat, or a bright-colored flower. You can make a hook from a bent pin or a bit of steel wire.

Another alternative is to catch fish with your hands, but this is noisy, messy, requires a specialized upbringing, and generally is not advised.

Gut the fish and cook them either in a pan (if you have one) or threaded on a skewer. Season with herbs and potatoes, which you may find growing in the Wild or in someone's garden.

Knot Tying

Ropes and their use are basic to survival in the Wild. You may find it necessary to climb up or down a mountainside, secure a boat, or simply use a bit of rope to tie items onto your pack. In any case, you'll need a basic knowledge of knot craft. Practice tying the following kinds of knots:

- **HITCH.** Used to fasten a rope to a post or a pinnacle of rock. It can either be fixed or sliding (if you want the knot to tighten when you pull on the rope).
- **LOOP.** Holds tightly around any object. Excellent for tying up packs so they don't come apart while you're running away from goblins, wargs, or balrogs.
- **BENDS.** These knots fasten two ropes together—helpful when you have several short ropes and need to climb down a particularly steep and high cliff face.

The best kinds of ropes are made by the elves; those of Lothlórien are particularly skilled in this art. Further, elven ropes have a tendency to come when you call, a useful quality if you don't want to leave a rope as a sure sign to pursuers that this is the way their prey came. Fifty ells of rope is a good length for the adventurer to carry; it should answer for most emergencies.

Swimming and Boating

Hobbits are sadly deficient in these skills (except for those who live near the banks of the Brandywine River). But swimming and boating are likely to come in handy if you're exploring a world penetrated by rivers, lakes, and inland seas. Traveling by boat is faster, safer, and more comfortable than walking or even riding, but if your boat overturns in rapids (or because, in a moment of panic, you grab for the edge of the boat and tip it over), you must know how to at least keep your head above water until a more skillful swimmer can reach you and propel you to shore. Above all, when in water, don't panic. Waving and shouting will only make you sink faster and perhaps attract unwelcome attention from the enemy.

Weapons and Their Uses

Any discussion of surviving in the Wild would be incomplete without a short lesson on how to use various weapons available to the adventurer. The average traveler is probably carrying a sword and possibly a bow, but these are not the only options. Here are some of the weapons available to you, together with comments on their usage.

Swords

This is the weapon de rigueur of anyone setting out for the Lands Beyond. Swords come in different lengths and weights, and the trick is to find one that you're comfortable wielding that also does some significant damage to anything it hits. A basic rule of thumb is that your sword should not be more than half your height. You should swing it easily with one hand, although two will put more force into the blow. Remember that sword fighting isn't a matter of wild slashing. The clever fighter uses the first moments of a battle to gauge his enemy's weaknesses and look for where blows will be successful. Parry, thrust, parry, thrust ... that's the rhythm to establish. Keep your sword sharp at all times, and remember to clean it thoroughly after you've killed someone. In the heat of battle, with multiple enemies, the cleaning will have to wait.

Hobbits often use daggers as swords, given their lack of height. That's fine, keeping in mind of course that a dagger or short sword used by a hobbit will do proportionally less damage to an opponent than a sword wielded by a full-sized human.

Shield

In addition to blocking your enemies' blows, you can use your shield itself as a weapon, thrusting it forward and knocking your opponent off balance. As with the sword, a shield should be comfortable to carry. Some come with a spike (or boss) in the middle, also useful as an offensive weapon. Shields are also helpful for sleighing down snowy slopes or skidding down a flight of stairs while firing arrows at the enemy.

Bow and Arrow

This is an excellent weapon for those venturing into the unknown. Its light, portable arrows are retrievable (at least in most circumstances; if they hit an oliphaunt, it's probably a good idea to let them go), and it kills almost silently. It requires a good deal of practice, but once mastered, it's essential to the equipment of any adventurer. Practice firing rapidly and smoothly, and try to retrieve as many arrows as you can; they're expensive and time-consuming to make, and in all probability, you won't replenish your store until you touch base with civilization again.

Axe

These are the preferred weapons of dwarves, although dwarves are also known to carry swords (Thorin Oakenshield, for instance, wielded the sword Orcrist, and upon his death in the Battle of Five Armies, it was placed on his tomb under the Lonely Mountain). The skilled dwarf can slice a goblin's head off with a stroke of an axe and decapitate another with the backswing. Since dwarves are short, their strokes are likely to disembowel a taller opponent (a troll, for instance) or take out a pair of kneecaps.

Crossbow

These are handy during sieges but less useful as portable weapons.
For one thing, they're laborious to load and crank to firing position.
Although a crossbow bolt is potentially more dangerous than an
arrow (it can, for instance, penetrate most armor, except *mithril*),
its effectiveness is mainly in massed fire from ramparts against
the serried ranks of the enemy. Still, some adventurers take them
on long journeys.

Stones

These are plentiful, handy, and deadly against spiders, though
not much else. Still, a well-thrown stone can knock down even an
armored knight, although he'll probably be back on his feet in a few
minutes with a headache and a permanent grudge against whoever
was unsporting enough to pitch a rock at him. On the whole, stones
are best confined to opponents who are the size of giant spiders or
smaller. Hobbits are adept at this sort of weapon, having practiced at
the dartboard of their local pub.

Guides to the Lands of the Wild

It's called the Wild for a reason: You won't find many guides to it,
and those that exist are often out of date and unreliable. Still, if
you're bound and determined to be better prepared before setting out, there are a couple of possible aids that will minimize the
chance of you becoming completely lost and spending weeks traveling in circles.

Maps

The elves are big on maps, and many of the best maps of Middle-
earth are made by elves. Being elves, they delight in offering cryptic, hard-to-understand instructions along the lines of "Here be ye
great dangers! Mortals beware!" They also like to use such things as
moon letters, which is secret writing that only appears on the map

when the full moon is shining behind it (at which point it's probably far too late to do the owner of the map any good at all).

Dwarves also make maps, which are a good deal more practical than those made by elves. Dwarvish maps tend to show mines, secret doors to mines, important chambers in mines, and the location of taverns, based on the excellence of the ale served.

Hobbit maps are a bit like hobbits themselves: They wander around a lot and often don't go anywhere in particular, but they enjoy themselves while they're getting there.

Rangers

Rangers are useful guides for explaining the perils and possibilities of the road ahead. That's because, being Rangers, they, well, range. That is, they spend most of their time on the road, exploring, so they're more likely to have an accurate idea of what's out there than most maps. The downside is that Rangers are:

- Taciturn
- Gloomy
- Cranky
- Disinclined to talk to anyone they deem frivolous—or, at any rate, less serious about the state of the world than they are, which is pretty much everyone

Old Men Who Sit By the Tavern Fire, Muttering to Themselves

Such men can be persuaded to speak after you've bought them three or four pints of their favorite ale. Keeping in mind what it takes to gain information from them, you should have an idea of how reliable that information is likely to be.

Innkeepers

Practically useless as sources of information, innkeepers hear a lot of gossip from travelers, but since they're constantly rushing about carrying mugs of ale and wine, they only hear half of what's being said and remember only a quarter of that. Thus they constantly get things mixed up and spew out the results as a kind of stew of misinformation. As a general rule, if a landlord tells you to do something while on the road, play it safe and do the opposite.

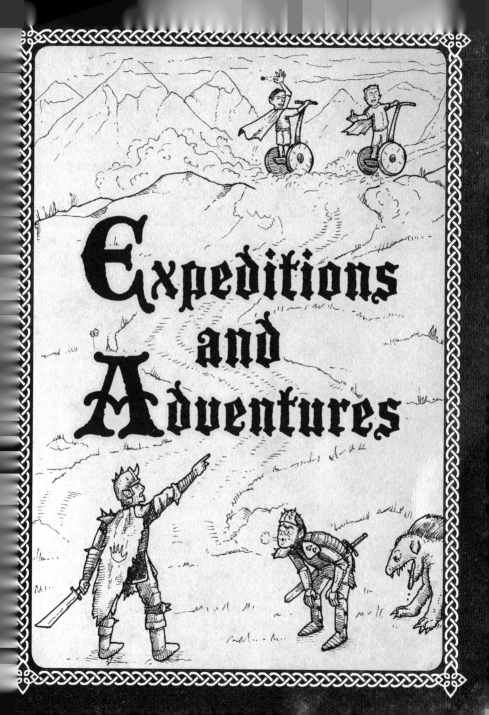

arriors are busy fighting one another in distant lands, and in this neighborhood heroes are scarce, or simply not to be found. Swords in these parts are mostly blunt, and axes are used for trees, and shields as cradles or dish-covers; and dragons are comfortably far-off (and therefore legendary)."

—Gandalf in JRR Tolkien's *The Hobbit*

When Bilbo ran down the lane toward the Green Dragon, without his pocket handkerchief or his pipe and pipeweed, he was taking a step into a much larger world than he'd ever imagined existed. It wasn't just a change in the physical scenery that mattered. It was a change in his mental scenery as well. He admitted that as the adventure (or Adventure, as he tended to think of it) went on, he found himself assuming a role that he never would have imagined possible when the uninvited dwarves first gathered in his parlor at Bag End.

In the battle with the spiders of Mirkwood, he found himself, involuntarily, the leader of the dwarves, ready, as he himself said, to "do the stinging." It was he who rescued the hapless dwarves from the wiles of the spiders; it was he who found an escape from the dungeons of the Wood-Elves; it was he, at last, who discovered the "back door" into the Lonely Mountain and the path to the treasure hoard of Smaug the dragon.

Even when he and the dwarves first arrived at the Lonely Mountain and were sitting outside the "back door" waiting for something to happen, Bilbo was a far different hobbit than the funny little fellow "bobbing on the door mat," who had run out of Bag End without a pocket handkerchief. Gazing over the deserted town of Esgaroth, he dangled his feet and stared into the distance beyond the wood and mountains, wondering about the distant lands just over the horizon and what adventures they held.

Frodo and his friends had far more of those adventures than they bargained for, and for Frodo at least, it was a great relief to return to his old familiar haunts in the Shire—even though they were altered and he himself would spend only a few years there before taking sail from the Gray Havens for the Undying West.

Many of us are like that—we don't expect adventures, and we resist them when they knock at our doors. But after all, we need them to spur us into the lands beyond our Shires, lands holding the promise of new experiences and new wonders to behold.

For some hobbits—Bilbo and those brave adventurers who come after him—the lands beyond the fields they know are a constant temptation.

Mode of Travel

For a hobbit, the preferred means of travel is his own woolly feet. Although Bilbo and the dwarves occasionally travel by pony, they walk a good part of the way to the Lonely Mountain. Of course, eagles also carry them some of the way.

Travel Maintenance

Ponies are all well and good when you can get them, and Bilbo and the dwarves begin their journey on a nice group of young horses that last as far as Rivendell. On the other hand, there's the matter of stabling them, grazing them, and (in the interests of stealth) picking up after them. Perhaps walking isn't so bad after all. Walkers should be sure to equip themselves with sturdy packs and stout staves, helpful for picking one's way amid ruts and boulders in the road as well as for fighting off the odd goblin attack.

Walking the Paths of the Wild

One's own feet are the most reliable means of transportation, but that isn't to say that they're the most convenient. After all, walking is slow, treacherous, and subject to weather and occasional attacks by midges, spiders (big and small), and Dark Riders. Still, on foot, you can expect to go about two or three miles per hour, which for a full day of walking will take you fifteen or twenty miles closer to your destination. And, among other things, it will improve your physique. Frodo is twice the hobbit he was when he and his friends finally arrive at Rivendell, ready to start the next, and longer, stage of his quest.

Travel by Ent

Pippin and Merry are the only two hobbits to travel via Ent—an unusual but highly efficient mode of transportation. Pippin goes so far as to try to count Ent strides (getting lost at about three thousand). Assuming most Ents are about as tall as Treebeard (fourteen feet high) and that the average Ent stride is about four and a half feet, three-thousand Ent strides would run to only about two and a half miles. In reality, Ents probably walk much further than that. We can reasonably assume that Ents travel at about twelve or thirteen miles per hour and are easily able to walk a hundred miles in a day. For purposes of travel in a place the size of Middle-earth, that's a good pace.

Travel by Boat

Keep in mind, of course, that hobbits generally dislike water. Hobbits, as we learn early on, come in three varieties: Stoors, Fallohides, and Harfoots. Of these, only Stoors (from whom were descended most of the Brandybucks and hobbits of Buckland) had any interest in, or skill with, boats. Hobbits in general distrust boats as nasty, tricky things, as likely to dump you into the water and drown you as not. However, when push comes to shove, a hobbit will travel by water, although he won't be happy about it. Sam Gamgee, about as typical a hobbit as you'll find outside the Shire, complains constantly when traveling by boat down the Anduin River, and the others of the Fellowship learn quickly that he's not to be trusted with a paddle, even in calm waters. So travel by boat is an option, but only in the most desperate of circumstances.

Warg in Waiting

Those of the goblin (or orc) persuasion may want to consider riding wargs. The wild wolves of Middle-earth have the minor drawback of occasionally eating their passengers (and anything else that gets in their way), but surely that's a minor inconvenience compared to the security of riding your own private, living tank. Wargs have a wide range and are quite capable of devouring the irritating dwarf, elf, or hobbit that gets in your way. (Special note: Beware of wizards wielding staffs!) (Extra-special note: Beware of elves wielding bows!)

Fly the Friendly Skies

If neither pony nor foot nor boat nor Ent will serve, consider asking an eagle for a lift. The advantage: a bird's-eye view of the landscape of Middle-earth. The disadvantage? Well, slipping off midflight, for one thing. For another, there's always the danger that the eagle will mistake you for a morsel intended for one of its offspring. But that's a small price to pay for a quick flight. Eagles are discerning birds with a general allegiance to the right side in a fight, but it's all too possible for an eagle, on an early morning reconnaissance flight, to mistake a hobbit for a tasty rabbit. The general lesson: Eagles are useful but potentially dangerous allies.

Appropriate Clothing

If you're going to go off on a quest, for goodness sake dress the part! For example, when traveling for a long journey in varying weather, something simple in a dark green hood and cloak is indicated. If one is cautiously stealing into the heart of a dragon's lair, it's better to wear something sturdier—*mithril* mail perhaps. Above all, wear boots. They're a good indication of how long you've been traveling (Strider's are caked with mud when Frodo first meets him), as well as your status as an adventurer.

Equipment

Questing is a dangerous business, and one should not undertake it lightly. The basic equipment one might take when setting off in search of a dragon-guarded treasure includes the following:

- A sword
- A coat of mail—preferably dragon-proof
- A cloak
- Rope, because you never know when it'll come in handy; if you don't have it, you'll want it
- Boots (unless you're a hobbit, in which case, fur-shod feet will serve)
- A magic ring that makes you invisible (optional but helpful)

Keep in mind that at least half, if not two-thirds, of your equipment will be lost along the way in misadventures, encounters with trolls, dragon attacks, and disastrous adventures involving goblins and wargs. So plan to take at least twice as much of anything you need, since someone else will wind up with half of it before your adventure's over.

Things Not to Take With You

Lest you be tempted to over-equip yourself with items you really won't need on an expedition in search of adventure, here are some things not to take with you:

- **MUSICAL INSTRUMENTS.** It's true that at the beginning of the adventure you might want to sing a long, epic song that explains to anyone who cares to listen how you came to be in the fix you're in and why the treasure buried under the mountain is yours. But are you really going to need clarinets, bass viols, a drum, flutes, fiddles, and a harp for all that? And what are you going to do with all of these musical instruments when your party is attacked by goblins in the mountains? Better leave it all at home and practice your a capella singing.
- **COOKING EQUIPMENT.** Keep in mind that you're going to be traveling through the Wild, where food will mostly consist of game shot with arrows and slow roasted over an open fire. No one's going to care whether you can sauté a rabbit or fricassee a pigeon. A box of salt is nice; salt is always useful. Leave the pots and pans at home.
- **GOLD AND SILVER.** This applies particularly when you're coming home from a quest. You're traveling through a lot of lawless lands, without any particular protection (unless you travel with a wizard, then you're probably all right). Gold and silver attract thieves—try a letter of credit instead. You can still pay for first-class accommodations at inns along the way.

Weapons

Hobbits are especially good with anything that can be thrown: stones, darts, quoits, and so forth. Elves, on the other hand, are skilled bowmen, able to hit a target a long ways distant while slipping from tree to tree. Dwarves, as implied in Gimli's case (and reinforced by Dáin and other dwarves), prefer axes. Wizards such as Gandalf and Saruman use their staves (and, occasionally, swords). Men such as Aragorn and Boromir prefer swords—not merely swords but named swords that have a lineage. For example, Aragorn carries Andúril, the Flame of the West, the Sword That Was Broken and Has Been Reforged. That's a pretty impressive lineage for a sword, and you have to wonder if Anduril would have preferred being called Smith or Jones or something a bit less epic.

Using Rope

When traveling, it's possible—nay, probable—that you'll have to use a rope somewhere for something. In that case, remember the following points:

- **THE MORE ROPE YOU HAVE WITH YOU, THE BETTER.** After all, it's not possible, when climbing down a steep cliff face, to have more than enough rope.
- **HAVING SOMEONE IN THE PARTY WHO CAN TIE KNOTS IS A VERY GOOD IDEA.** Simple clove hitches are essential to any good traveling party, but if you have someone who knows a splice from a bowline and who can tie a square knot without getting the ends mixed up, well, you're golden.
- **GOOD ROPE COMES WHEN IT'S CALLED.** If you tie a strong knot and lower yourself down, then call the rope to come after you, chances are it'll do it. Of course, it helps if the rope was made by elves originally.
- **ROPE IS GOOD FOR MANY THINGS.** For instance, you can use it to climb down a cliff, climb up a cliff, guide your way through a maze, or in desperate straits, secure a nasty, slimy creature that's been following you for weeks.

Food and Drink

Bilbo says little or nothing about the inns the party uses after they leave the Shire. However, travelers are well advised to keep an eye peeled for well-kept, neat, pleasant establishments. The Prancing Pony in Bree is highly recommended, since it caters to both men and hobbits. Perigrine Took makes reference to The Golden Perch in Stock in the Shire. In such a house, one desires a pleasant common room, good beer, plain fare, and soft, clean, inviting beds. An absence of Black Riders also makes for a good night's sleep.

Ale

The best beer may be in the East Farthing (as Sam Gamgee knows), but there's no reason to turn up one's nose at other ales one is offered along the way. The discerning hobbit knows that beer is, after all, beer, and it's quite possible that the cellars of Minas Tirith may have as much to offer as the Green Dragon in Bywater. Still, hobbits and dwarves excel at the brewing of beer, while wine is the preferred drink of men and elves. Drunkenness is nothing to be ashamed of, provided it's cheerful and conducted in a lively company.

Brewing

Hobbits are surely among the earliest of craft brewers. The Golden Perch in East Farthing has excellent beer (Pippin recommended it to Sam), and presumably the Green Dragon has its own ale that's widely boasted of—widely known, at any rate—to attract a crowd from around the Shire. Sadly, no manual of Shire brews exists. (Meriadoc Brandybuck was public spirited enough to write a treatise on pipe-weed, but unfortunately, nothing on beer.) However, we can assume from stories passed from one generation to the next that a number of Shire inhabitants were well experienced in the art of brewing various kinds of beer, including ale, stout, lager, pilsner, and probably (given Tolkien), India Pale Ale. God knows what they called the latter: probably Anduin Pale Ale or something.

Eating With Hobbits

Hobbits are fond of good plain food—and plenty of it. Second breakfasts (and lunches, teas, and dinners) are common among them. Hobbits believe that if it can't be eaten, it doesn't have much of a point (excepting, of course, friendship and pipeweed). Normal hobbit meals include such fare as bread, tarts, mushrooms (in abundance), cheese, meats, pies, fruit, and as much wine and ale as can decently be drunk. Hobbits adore that moment in a dinner when one is mostly full but sits around the table, nibbling at the remaining fare, and "filling up the corners." And, of course, there's nothing better after dinner than a long pipe and a good nap.

Eating With the Elves

If you love meat and are never satisfied with a meal unless it contains a juicy, thick cut of steak, well, don't break bread with the elves. The Fair Folk are, for the most part, vegetarian. Their meals consist of bread, fruit, nuts, and wine, as well as mysterious drinks that aren't wine, aren't water, and yet set everyone's tongues wagging. The best thing to do when dining with elves is to eat plenty of everything. It may not be substantial, but it will salve your hunger better than many a hearty dinner in the Shire.

LANGUAGE TIPS

The elves of Middle-earth are not linguistically homogeneous. In fact, they have a variety of languages, depending on where they're from. For the most part, their dialects are sufficiently similar to one another that they can understand each other (the elves of Lothlórien have no difficulty in understanding Legolas Greenleaf, although he comes from Mirkwood, far to the north). Elf language, broadly speaking, is either Sindar or Quenya.

Lembas Waybread

The dwarves have *cram*; the elves have lembas. There's really no comparison: lembas keeps a strong warrior on his feet for several days, while *cram* is nothing more than English public school stodge. It's possible that the elves took *cram* and developed it into lembas; we really have no way of knowing the origins of this delicious yet nutritious sustenance. In any case, with a food bag full of lembas, anyone in Middle-earth can face a long journey with equanimity.

Eating With the Dwarves

Dwarf cuisine is unquestionably closer to hobbit tastes—and quite possibly most humans—than that of the elves. At least the dwarves eat meat! And drink beer! In large quantities! Then again, when you're traveling on a long journey you'd much rather be carrying a supply of lembas, the elvish waybread, than the dwarvish *cram* (which, as Bilbo quite rightly complains, sticks in one's throat). Dwarves, accustomed to long marches and privations, take pride in existing on short rations, something no hobbit would tolerate for a moment.

Eating With Men

From a hobbit's standpoint, eating with men is the most natural option. Hobbits like good plain food—simple dishes like steak and kidney pie, ripe cheeses, tarts, and a lot of ale to wash it down with. Apart from Númenóreans and those who "live on the heights," most men of Middle-earth would feel quite at home in a hobbit establishment such as the Green Dragon—and vice versa. The men of Minas Tirith eat bread, cheese, apples, and skins of ale, enough to satisfy for the time being the appetite of a hungry hobbit.

Meat

Though hobbits rarely eat meat, they won't turn their noses up at a nice bit of steak, even if it's cooked over an open fire on a forked stick. Possibly some venison, shot in the Wild by a helpful Ranger, would be welcome. Raccoon, possum, beaver, and rat also count for possibilities. Oh, all right! Not necessarily rat. Although it's welcome in times of famine—if not delicious, then at least nutritious. It tastes somewhat like chicken.

Manners

Hobbits, whatever their background, have been raised with proper manners. Despite being in Ithilien, many miles from home, Frodo and Sam know enough to follow the dinner customs of their hosts, and rise and bow to the west before beginning the meal. Frodo comments that he and Sam feel a bit rustic, even in their simple surroundings, observing the customs of Faramir and the men he commands. On the other hand, as Tolkien reminds his readers, it doesn't cost anything to observe good manners. When the dwarves unexpectedly call on Bilbo at the beginning of *The Hobbit* they tell him, "At your service." He remembers to reply, "At yours and your family's." It's a small gesture, but no doubt much appreciated.

Entertainment

Entertainment during meals isn't expected, but it's a nice variation. Be prepared, as part of the dinner menu, to tell the story of your travels, accompanied by songs, dancing, and possibly magic tricks. If one of you has a magical ring that makes the wearer vanish, well, that's an added bonus.

Comic Songs

Should you be asked to provide entertainment at a gathering, comic songs are not advisable. After all, one's idea of humor varies widely, and what strikes hobbits as amusing is more likely to impress a steward of Gondor as outrageously forthright or unbearably rustic. On the other hand, if you know a piece of historical or mythological poetry that you could recite, it's not likely to offend anyone. Just make sure you remember which side is supposed to win at the end.

Visiting Abroad

Hobbits don't, as a rule, stray far from home. But for those who do, certain rules apply:

- Adapt to local customs

1. Thank your guests properly before disappearing.
2. Don't regift presents, even *mathoms* (see below) that have circulated several times around the district. It's still rude.
3. Remember the proper names of those you've invited to attend. It's not Proudfoots, it's Proudfeet.
4. The proper way to say "Thank you" at a banquet is something along the lines of "Thank you very much for coming to my little party." It's not "Thag kew very budge." Even if you have a cold.

LANGUAGE TIPS

Mathoms

The hobbits of the Shire were fond of gift giving and give presents on their birthdays to all and sundry. Given the size of the population and the general practice of interfamilial marriage, most hobbits are related to one another, which means a lot of birthday parties and, consequently, a lot of present giving.

It's only natural that not all presents are equally valued. The hobbits consequently developed a term for presents that are "regifted"—in some cases they were passed around the Shire two or three times before finally settling into some unhappy household. The hobbit term for such gifts is *mathom*.

Although there is no modern English equivalent, the closest we can come to this term today is *fruitcake*.

When Visiting on the Heights

Cities are nervous sorts of places, with lots of people rubbing elbows with one another at far closer quarters than your average hobbit is used to. Whether built of stone or of wood, cities are unaccustomed

- Stay close to the ground in the event of a battle
- Do not meddle in the affairs of wizards, for they are subtle and quick to anger
- Do not meddle in the affairs of men, for they are long-winded and irrational
- Do not meddle in the affairs of dragons, for they find you delicious
- Oh, and as a final piece of advice: Keep plenty of pipeweed about. You never know when you'll need it.

Foreign Customs

When traveling in foreign parts, one should assume that the customs of the inhabitants will be different from what a well-bred hobbit is used to. Bilbo is no doubt pleasantly surprised to find that the men of Dale hold banquets on special occasions, just as the hobbits of the Shire do every midsummer's eve. After the destruction of the Ring, the men of Minas Tirith hold banquets and feasts as well, so no doubt Frodo and his companions are well feted.

Banquets

While the elves of Rivendell feast on occasion and spend many hours in the Hall of Fire telling stories and singing songs, hobbits, as Bilbo remarks, will never quite acquire the elvish taste for song and poetry. Still, the hobbits enjoy banquets, and there's nothing wrong with marking a special occasion with a feast. After all, the hobbits of the Shire, every midsummer's eve, hold a special banquet to elect the mayor of the Fourth Farthings, a post Will Whitflour has held at the beginning of *The Lord of the Rings* for some time.

Birthdays

Birthdays are best celebrated in the comfort of one's own home, and in the presence of friends, relatives, and a few specially invited wizards and dwarves. However, it may be that you'll find yourself celebrating birthdays abroad in strange, faraway places. In that case:

places for hobbits to live in. Nonetheless, it's always possible to find an inn that serves good beer. The lesson is: Adapt to circumstances.

Be Careful What You Say

If, by chance, you're visiting a city and are brought before the lord of the city, don't be too quick to volunteer for his service. You never can tell what this will get you. It's entirely possible that a few injudiciously chosen words on your part will place you squarely in the middle of an army going to attack the Dark Lord's tower. And no one wants that.

Make Friends With the People Who Know Where Food Is

Nothing is more important than breakfast—with the possible exception of second breakfast. A soldier ever goes in search of his next meal, and small men (or hobbits) may do mighty deeds at the table. The most important thing, therefore, when entering a new city, is to find out where the grub is coming from. It's possible that there's a well-ordered system—for instance, military kitchens (butteries)—that serve regular food. In that case, you'd be well advised to discover very quickly where they are, when meals are served, and what the portions are like.

Make Friends With the People Who Know Where the Drink Is, Too

Second only to knowing where your next meal is coming from is discovering who's serving the next drink. You may have to snatch it from under someone's nose or quietly extract it when his back is turned, but drink is essential to the enjoyment of any good round of food. Here's a general guide to drinking:

1. Beer, from a hobbit's point of view, is what they drink in Valinor.
2. Wine is great when you can't get beer.

3. Wine and beer together make a party much more fun; what could be better than an evening at the Prancing Pony in Bree, fueled by wine and beer?

4. If you can't get wine and you can't get beer, you're probably in Mordor (Sauron, apparently, doesn't believe in giving his troops alcohol; life must be pretty freaking boring if you work for the Dark Lord).

5. Interestingly, the first thing Saruman does when he takes over the Shire is to stop the brewing of beer, which probably says something about the hobbits' idea of Hell.

When in the High Places

Hobbits may not do well in high places (such as mountains, eagle eyries, and high staircases), but they recover once they return to the level plains and hole dwellings in Hobbiton and the Shire. The truth is that most of us (hobbits included) do better in our natural environments. If you're frightened by the circumstances in which you find yourself, always remember that sooner or later you move from the high places to the low ones, from the open, empty shelves of windy mountains to the secure burrows and comforting, panel-lined homes of the Shire.

If You Find Yourself Talking to People Who Think They're Better Than You

The tone you should use is the same one you use when people want to borrow money from you. Use a tone that is firm yet dignified, calm, yet cold and concise, assured yet accommodating. Above all, let these people know you're in control of the situation. They may think that they've got you besieged in a mountain with your dwarven companions, but you still have a trick or two to play. There's no way they're going to turn down the Arkenstone of Thráin.

Have a Bargaining Chip

This is the key to winning any negotiation: Have something the other side wants far more than what they're willing to give. Like Bilbo, you may have to be a bit underhanded in getting it, but once you have it under your cloak, you can use it to bargain your way out of just about any situation. Remember, the Arkenstone is the key to controlling any situation with people whose motives you're not quite sure of.

When in Eagles' Nests

If you wake up in an eagle's nest and the eagle is sitting near you, trimming its feathers, the best thing you can do is agree with whatever it says. Or does. I mean, it's not as if the situation's going to work out well for you, if you start arguing with it.

Eat What You're Given

If an eagle (or anybody else in a similar position) offers you something to eat, take it. It's not as if you're likely to be offered something better. And even though rabbit or pigeon roasted over an open fire may not be your idea of haute cuisine, it's much better than starving to death.

If You Have a Chance to Do an Eagle a Favor...

If you're casually sitting under a tree, thinking of this and that and not paying much attention to the world around you, and an eagle drops by with an arrow in its wing, promptly remove it. Trust me, it'll work out for the best in the end. A grateful eagle is one you want on your side. He'll at least be more willing to do you a lot of favors. He might even rescue you from the middle of Mordor just as Mount Doom is erupting.

When in Woods

Woods are comfortable. Woods are places where hobbits can be happy and frolic. Hobbits have a natural affinity for trees; they love everything that grows. Give the average hobbit a tree, a soft spot on the grass beneath its spreading branches, and a patch of sunshine, and he'll be asleep before you can say "Belladonna Took."

When in Big, Scary, Unknown Woods. And I'm Not Talking About Woods Anywhere Remotely Close to the Shire, But Woods That Are in a Completely Different Part of Middle-earth and Seem to Be Alive. That's How Scary They Are.

Make friends with the trees. Fast.

If the Trees Start Talking to You

Talk back. You don't want to be rude. Trees have feelings too, you know. And there's no reason to think they won't be able to give you valuable advice. They might even be able to offer significant support. Or overthrow a rogue wizard or two. Trees are very important allies.

If they offer you a drink—drink it. You can always buy a larger set of clothing.

If You're in a Live Wood

If the wood comes alive and offers you a drink, it's probably a good idea to accept. And if you find yourself very far from home and the wood is offering to take you to one of its halls, that's a good time to accept its hospitality as well. Who knows? You might like the drink it offers.

Accepting Drinks from Strange Trees

A tree that offers you drinks that taste like water on steroids is probably not something you'll encounter in the normal course of things. But if you do, drink the drink. It'll increase your height, weight, strength, and sexual stamina. You'll come home taller than everyone else. And you'll be able to tell other people in bars that you met the Oldest Living Thing Ever. That's got to be good for a few rounds of ale.

If You See a Fire Among the Trees

If something glows a long way off in the distance and it looks like a fire, but you've been warned not to leave the path under any circumstances, no matter what you see, even if it looks like a fire and you're starving and tired and hungry and you don't really care anymore about your quest, and you wonder if they've got honey cakes and mead and ale wherever they're eating way back among the trees and you really, really, *really* want to go and investigate. Don't. Trust me. It won't end well.

Just Who Lives in Woods?

Lots of nasty creatures make their homes in the woods. These include, but are not limited to, the following:

- **TROLLS.** Stone trolls aren't very bright and can easily be fooled, but once they've got their hands on you they're not likely to let go. They like to eat anything that moves, including men, elves, dwarves, and hobbits (when they can recognize them). To render them helpless, wait until dawn, when they'll turn to stone.

- **SPIDERS.** Ordinary-sized spiders exist, of course, in abundance, but in the darker, more remote sections of the forest, you'll find the descendants of Ungoliant, ready to feast on fresh blood. They're larger than men (even pretty big men) and equipped with stingers that will render smaller creatures helpless. They prefer their meat fresh, having hung it head down for a couple of days. To defend against such spiders, have plenty of stones and an assortment of insulting names handy.

- **GOBLINS.** Let's face it: Goblins are pretty much everywhere
  you find darkness, damp, gloom, and mold. They have swords,
  fire, and an appetite for ponies. I mean, *they eat ponies!* What
  else do they eat? Fluffy kittens? Baby ducks? Elmo? To defend
  against them, you need magic goblin-killing swords and a spell
  that produces fire from nothing.

- **WOOD-ELVES.** All right, Wood-elves aren't nasty. They're
  just … unreliable. Like most elves, they have a somewhat
  exaggerated opinion of their own importance, and they're
  suspicious of nearly all strangers, no matter how innocent.
  They don't treat their prisoners badly, compared to the
  way goblins treat prisoners, but still, they keep prisoners
  in cells underground.

When in Caves

Compared to some of the really unsavory places you may find in
Middle-earth, caves aren't too bad. Hobbits are fond of holes, really,
and caves are just very long, deep holes. However, when caves are
inhabited by goblins and other, nastier things, they can be problem-
atic. Be sure to find the exit as quickly as possible. You don't have
to use it right away, but at least know where it is.

If You Meet Something in a Cave That's Lived There for a Really, Really Long Time...

Caves are places where dark, mysterious things dwell. Slimy, dark,
mysterious things. With big, pointy teeth. If you meet one of them,
it's probably as well to find something to pass the time. Possibly a
riddle game. Yeah, that's it. A riddle game. Because dark slimy things
always like riddles.

Hobbits and dwarves are more comfortable in caves than, say,
elves (except the Wood-elves of Mirkwood, and they are a special
case). The main thing to keep in mind is to keep going up. Going

down in a cave gets you into all sorts of places you'd rather not be. Going up gets you closer to the light and back doors, which are both very good things.

Stalagmites and Stalactites

Caves are full of mysterious protrusions that grow from the floor and from the ceiling. Lots of people confuse the two, but it's pretty simple to keep them straight. A stalactite hangs from the ceiling (it has to hold "tight" to the ceiling of a cave). A stalagmite grows from the floor (it takes a lot of "might" to grow upward). In either case, stalagmites and stalactites can be handy places to hide from the prying eyes of strange creatures that want to eat you.

The Woods and the Mountains

When traveling between the mountains and the woods, keep an eye out for:

- **PARTIES OF ROVING WARGS AND GOBLINS.** This sort of thing is seasonal. Summer is a popular time for raiding parties—the days are warm, the light stays longer, and all the woodsmen are busy getting drunk. What better time for wargs and goblins to team up and eat a few villages?
- **EAGLES.** Eagles like to hunt at night, and even though their eyesight is extremely keen, it's entirely possible that a large economy-size eagle will mistake an innocent traveler for dinner. Consider waving a primitive flag or making a hand signal to show you're not a wayward rabbit, just an innocent wayfarer who wants to be left in peace.
- **SHAPE CHANGERS.** Bears are bad enough. Bears that change into humans that pretend to be bears are even worse. The technical term for creatures like this is were-bears, but shape changers will do. They're dangerous, but they can be useful

allies, particularly against goblins and wargs. The chief lesson you can learn from were-bears is that you shouldn't judge a book by its cover or an ally by its skin. Remember: Some of the best and stoutest allies have fur.

Crossing Water

Essentially there are two ways to cross a body of water: by swimming or by boat. If you can't swim (and almost no hobbits can), you can try a boat. If you don't like boats (and few hobbits do), you can walk around the water or sit down and wait in hopes of something or someone coming along to carry you to the other side.

Cities

Hobbits much prefer towns to cities; the latter are too large and too populated for comfort. However, hobbits can acclimate to just about anything, including cities. Fortunately, they're not called upon to do so very often. In the time of Frodo and Aragorn, Middle-earth had, effectively, only two cities: Minas Tirith, the guard against Mordor, and Minas Morgul, city of the Witch-king. Towns (such as Bree, Hobbiton, or the towns surrounding Gondor), settlements (such as Rivendell or Isengard), or military outposts (such as Osgiliath) were much more prevalent.

Finding Your Way About

Fortunately, cities in Middle-earth aren't that big or that complicated in their structure. Minas Tirith rises in seven concentric circles, each piercing the reef of rock at the easternmost point of the city. So even Pippin, who's new to Minas Tirith, doesn't have a lot of difficulty in navigating the city. He simply continues downward until he reaches the level of the gates; there's nowhere else to go.

Minas Morgul's geography is more difficult to estimate, but it's no larger than Minas Tirith—probably smaller, since the Ringwraiths don't require as much space to operate.

Food and Drink

Every big city has its taverns. Even smaller towns such as Hobbiton and Bywater offer places where a hungry and thirsty hobbit can settle down with a well-deserved sandwich and a pint. Minas Tirith may be a city of stone and tradition, but plenty of friendly pubs within its city walls will serve a pint to a warrior after a hard day's work of fighting off Nazgul. Take a lesson from hobbits: When entering a city, your first matter of business should be to find out where the grub is served.

Government

Hobbits, by and large, use simple governing structures. The Shire has a mayor, the Mayor of Michel Delving, elected once every seven years. His primary duty is to preside at banquets. Cities, on the other hand, are more complicated. Minas Tirith comes complete with a steward, at first, and later, a king. The latter's jurisdiction extends all the way to the Shire. (King Elessar eventually makes it a free province and forbids men to enter.) Even so, the hobbits maintain their traditional ways, seven times electing Samwise Gamgee mayor of the Shire. The kingship of Gondor continues, although the Shire may or may not still be part of its domain. In any case, the lesson of Shire politics is simply: "All politics is local."

Town Masters

The exception that proves the rule about local government seems to be the Master of Lake-town. His is an elected position, and it's clear that a certain amount of corruption accompanies it. Like most politicians, he's a proven coward, and he is willing to say anything to divert attention from his involvement in Esgaroth's deplorable situation following the dragon attack.

It's impossible to say how many other towns in Middle-earth have masters. The general rule of thumb is clear, though: Don't trust anyone who's elected (except the Mayor of Michel Delving, who's pretty harmless).

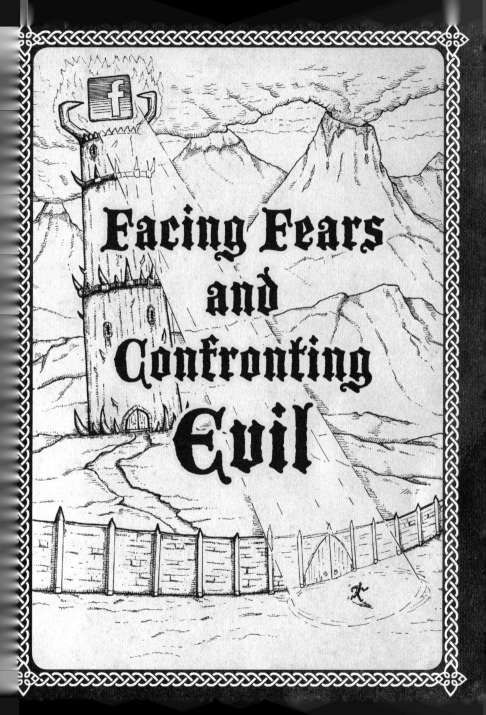

Facing Fears and Confronting Evil

've been in terror of you and your dogs for over thirty years, Farmer Maggot, though you may laugh to hear it. It's a pity: for I've missed a good friend."

—Frodo in JRR Tolkien's
The Fellowship of the Ring

Hobbits are small, and the world is big. There are monsters in Middle-earth, and most of these—indeed most everything in that world—are bigger than hobbits. Even all the hobbits together would not make an army of much significance, nor are there hobbit warlords who could stand toe-to-toe with orcs or cave trolls.

In a sense, hobbits are the children of Middle-earth. In their secluded Shire, they are blissfully unaware of the horrors and creatures that could destroy them in a day. Dark forces would've long ago crept into the Shire and ended its innocence had Strider's Rangers not kept their long vigil. The Rangers, like parents sheltering young children, strove to maintain the hobbits' isolation for as long as possible.

Because, for the hobbits, "growing up" would mean the death of something precious in the world.

It is natural for a child to be afraid of things. A healthy dose of fear keeps him from dangerous situations. Fear is an acknowledgment that something may be more powerful than oneself and that it could cause damage and should therefore be avoided or at least treated with great care.

Yet, even in the rarified preserve in which the hobbits live, some fears remain: fear of boats and drowning, fear of Gandalf's magical fireworks, fear of Farmer Maggot's dogs, fear of strange news from Bree. Just across the Hedge from Buckland lies the Old Forest, where there are indeed things to fear. And beyond that, the Barrow-downs, where no hobbit with any sense would ever go.

A person, young or old, who has never faced true fear does not know what he would do in a truly fearful situation. Some parts of one's character can be revealed only in a crisis. An argument can be made that, without fear, no person can reach his full potential. Certainly that is true of the hobbits who left the Shire in Tolkien's stories.

The greater world of Middle-earth, just like the world beyond a child's understanding, is filled with virtuous men, women, and other beings, but also with agents of terrible evil. All of us must reach childhood's end eventually. We must venture out from the protection of our upbringing and encounter the wide world. Because it is not inside the Shire where our true identities are to be found, but outside.

The (Hobbit) Hero's Journey

Both *The Hobbit* and *The Lord of the Rings* belong to a category of narrative called the hero's journey.

The hero's journey is a term coined by American mythologist Joseph Campbell to refer to the monomyth, the one basic narrative pattern that is found in nearly every culture and civilization throughout human history.

In *The Hero with a Thousand Faces*, Campbell laid out the phases of the hero's journey. They fall into three parts: departure, initiation, and return. These phases contained most or all of the following components:

Departure:
- The call to adventure (often brought by the "herald")
- Refusal of the call

- Supernatural aid
- The crossing of the first threshold
- Belly of the whale

Initiation:
- The road of trials (including new allies and enemies)
- The meeting with the goddess (a.k.a., mystical marriage)
- Woman as temptress
- Atonement with the father
- Apotheosis (elevation in rank to godhood)
- The ultimate boon

Return:
- Refusal of the return
- The magic flight
- Rescue from without
- The crossing of the return threshold
- Master of two worlds
- Freedom to live

The graphic on the next page depicts the journey, though with some added or altered terms.

Broadly speaking, the hero's journey is the story of 1) a hero (or heroine) who was safe and protected at home, perhaps spoiled and longing for adventure, who is 2) forced to go out into the scary outside world, where he meets many new challenges and allies but eventually overcomes them all to truly become a mighty warrior, and who then 3) returns home to bring to his people the fruit of what he's learned and achieved.

The application to *The Hobbit* is clear. Bilbo was the epitome of the spoiled and protected—and untried—innocent. He is cast out, quite against his will, into that terrifying unknown beyond the boundaries of his land. In this journey, he encounters new allies and enemies, gains a mentor, finds a magical talisman, and achieves heroic,

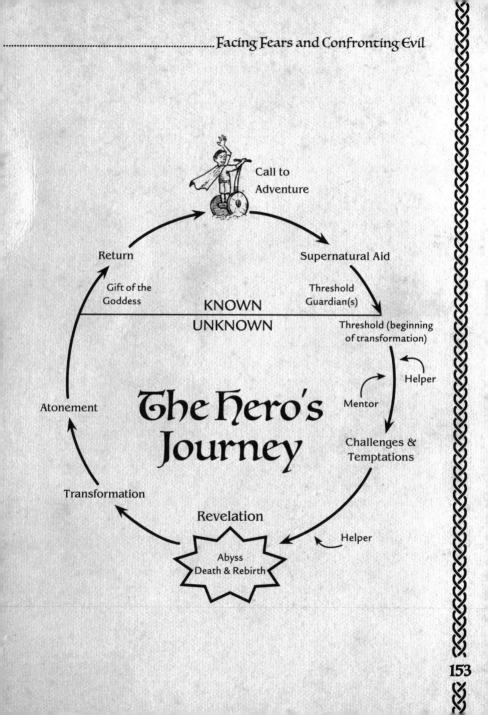

Call to
Adventure

Return

Supernatural Aid

Gift of the
Goddess

Threshold
Guardian(s)

KNOWN

UNKNOWN

Threshold (beginning
of transformation)

Helper

Atonement

Mentor

The Hero's
Journey

Challenges &
Temptations

Transformation

Revelation

Helper

Abyss
Death & Rebirth

grown-up things of which he never believed himself capable. In the end, he returns to the Shire with the riches won on his journey. But he is no longer the same. He is master of two worlds—those inside and outside the Shire—and prefers the company of elves and wizards to that of his fellow hobbits.

Frodo's journey in *The Lord of the Rings* follows the same pattern, though on a more epic scale. Many people wonder about the extended ending of the book version of *The Return of the King*. In a purely narrative sense, the story is essentially over when Sauron is defeated. All that is required is a return home to enjoy the peace and innocence the heroes have protected.

But from a hero's journey perspective, the story is not over until the heroes have returned home and brought to their families the wealth of what they have learned and become on their travels. They went out to war and became heroes. When they get home, they find that their heroism is in need once again. They lead the uprising against Sharky and achieve the Scouring of the Shire.

Had they never gone on their journey, no one would have opposed Sharky and his minions, and the Shire would've been surely enslaved. Frodo, Sam, Merry, and Pippin would've been herded to their doom like all the rest of the hobbits. But they are heroes now, and dark times call for heroes.

Tolkien wrote hero's journey tales. Certainly he didn't rely on Joseph Campbell's work directly, since *The Hero with a Thousand Faces* wasn't published until 1949 and *The Hobbit* was published in 1937. But Campbell's genius was to recognize the monomyth in every culture and to condense the various components into a cohesive list, like the one found previously. Doubtless Tolkien sensed these steps inherently, as have so many others across every civilization throughout human history. It has even been argued that the hero's journey is a fingerprint of the divine.

Because, truly, it is man's story. We all start as children who are sheltered in some respect or another but who must eventually venture out into the frightening world of adulthood. Hopefully, while on this journey, we "grow up," we become individuated (to use Carl Jung's term), we finally "get it" and achieve a level of mastery that allows us to excel in our lives as confident adults. Finally, we bring what we have learned and apply it to the home, family, and community in which we choose to live.

Once you understand the phases and their components of the hero's journey, you'll begin to see it everywhere. At least half of the stories Hollywood and novelists produce are hero's journey stories. Examine *Star Wars, The Little Mermaid, Cars, Ender's Game, The Hurt Locker, The King's Speech, No Country for Old Men*, and many, many others, and you'll see the monomyth lying beneath. Indeed, George Lucas befriended Joseph Campbell and worked with him extensively to make *Star Wars* the quintessential hero's journey tale. Tolkien's narratives are no less hero's journey stories.

The Hero's Journey, Hobbits, Fear, and Evil

Psychologist Carl Jung would say that the hero's journey is the universal coming of age story, the road everyone must take if he or she is to reach fully realized adulthood, a process he called individuation.

If hobbits are the children of Middle-earth, then those sent out into the world—those who survive and return, anyway—are the first hobbit adults. They are sadder but wiser, acquainted with the ways of the world, able to teach and lead and equip a new generation, if anyone will listen.

In the world outside the Shire, there is fear and evil. A child might be protected from such things, but one who would mature must face them. Both Bilbo's and Frodo's stories are tales of untried neophytes facing fearful evil and gaining progressively greater levels of competency as a result.

Bilbo's fears of traveling beyond the borders of the Shire seemed well-founded when he and the dwarves—without Gandalf—encountered the three trolls roasting mutton. He was not far from home and already something wanted to eat him. Would have too, had Gandalf not come along.

Funny how Gandalf disappeared and reappeared at crucial times during Tolkien's tales. Had he been there all along, the hobbits in his care would never have learned for themselves the lessons of the road to heroism.

Stop for a moment and consider your own story. Can you recall any hard lesson that you learned only because no one was there to protect you or take care of it for you? Maybe a sibling or friend fell into deep water, and no adults were around. Maybe you were the only one to see the fire begin. Maybe the scorpion got in the house while you were alone.

All of us prefer to call on someone bigger, wiser, and stronger to protect us. That's natural. But sometimes the chain of possibilities ends with you. You are the last link. No one else is there. If the good is going to happen or the bad is going to be avoided, it's up to you.

Such moments are the birthplace of heroes.

Bilbo's Inner Journey

If you had to pick one theme that is at the heart of *The Hobbit*, it would probably have to be Bilbo's rise to heroism. Other themes have been suggested by analysts—like issues of race, lineage, and character—and certainly those are prominent in the book. But in the end, it is the story of Bilbo's transformation from spineless to fearless, from spectator to player, and from child to man.

Let's track his transformation. And perhaps ours, as well.

Plunging Into the Unknown

The first fear Bilbo had to confront was that of leaving his comfortable home and going on some random and obviously ill-fated "adventure." Why would he ever do such a thing? He wouldn't! Not if left to his own preferences.

Sometimes what we fear is simply the unknown. If you never leave your home, you can begin to think that other places are dangerous. One is reminded of the movie *The Truman Show*, in which the title character has been conditioned all his life to believe that life in his little town on his little island is the only source of safety in the world. Consequently, he is terrified to even think of leaving, though the outside calls to him on some level.

A certain woman was pregnant for the first time. At first, she was simply excited about this new life growing within her (when it wasn't making her sick). But as the months passed and the great deadline began to approach, her fears mounted. What would happen? What would it be like? Could something go wrong? She and her husband began to fill their great lack of knowledge with information: reading books, watching videos, talking to other new mothers, and more.

The idea of a frightening D-Day approaching inexorably is terrifying. But at least in pregnancy you have nine months to prepare for the event. What if in a single day you found out you were pregnant and due to give birth that very day? To have feared labor and delivery your whole life and then to have it happen right away would be even worse.

Such was Bilbo's situation. He'd always feared the world outside the Shire, and now, with no warning, he was thrust into it. Not with a handpicked band of trusted friends, either, but with strangers completely unlike himself. He might as well have been kidnapped by Vikings.

Even if he longed for an adventure, this wasn't the one he would have chosen. Not only was he not going of his own will, he was billed as a burglar, something he was most decidedly not. What was Gandalf doing to him? And why had he picked Bilbo, of all hobbits, to visit this curse upon?

Perhaps you have been through something similar. For years you'd feared some scenario, and then one day you were thrust into it, quite against your will. Were you drafted into something you didn't volunteer for? Did you deal with it more or less like Bilbo did? Kicking and screaming? Reasoning or bargaining? Chances are, you weren't able to get out of it.

Did anything good come of it? Did you gain anything from the experience, even though you hadn't chosen it? Some of our most important life lessons come when we're forced to do something we never would've chosen to do on our own.

Problems We Cause Ourselves

Bilbo hadn't been on the road with the dwarves long before he encountered the three trolls. Now he had something real to fear. Many times, the unknown is worse than what actually transpires. Other times, the thing that actually transpires will try to eat you.

In this case, it is Bilbo's cheekiness, not his timidity, that gets him into trouble. Had he just gone back to warn the dwarves of the trouble ahead, instead of trying to pinch a troll's coin purse, much grief would've been avoided.

Sometimes we, too, get into trouble we should've avoided. Perhaps it's because, like Bilbo, we're wanting to show off or prove something to someone. Maybe we're addicted to the adrenaline rush we get when we take a risk.

In an attempt to escape from the trolls, Bilbo uses his small size to hide, like a child forgotten in a tussle among adults. That's an unwitting beginning to his eventual practice of using his unheroic attributes to turn him not into a brawling warrior but a canny burglar.

But as Bilbo hides, the dwarves get trapped one by one, until it's just Bilbo and Thorin left.

Bilbo shows his first sign of heroism here, when he attempts to save Thorin by grabbing a troll on the leg. It was a foolish, futile gesture, but it came from a heart that was beginning to care about the others in his group. The fact that he was more or less the cause of them all getting caught probably accelerated his concern, but his little melee was still a step in a good direction.

What about you: Have you ever gotten into a fearful situation that you brought on yourself? Did it result in others getting hurt? Hopefully that's a lesson you won't need to repeat.

Cleverness in the Face of Fear

After a restful stay in Rivendell, Bilbo and the dwarves were off again on their quest toward the Lonely Mountain. But it's not long after that they are set upon by goblins and captured.

The farther from the Shire they travel, the greater the dangers become and the hardier the heroes must be to weather the journey.

So it is in our own lives: adulthood can be wonderful. Striking out on our own, forging our own identity, reinventing ourselves, coming into our own, forming a family the way we feel it should be done. But adulthood can also be a frightening realm. For most people, the transition from child to adult has nothing to do with physical age. There are sixty-year-old babies and eight-year-old elders, in a manner of speaking.

In our lives, as in the hero's journey—and in Bilbo's life—the deeper we go into the realm of adulthood, the more heroic we need to be. Pansies need not apply.

It is the school of fears and crises, and even failures, that brings out the hero in all of us.

Gandalf rescues Bilbo and the dwarves from the goblins, but in the battle, Bilbo is separated from the group and knocked unconscious. When he wakes up, he finds himself alone in a dark cave. He feels about on the floor and discovers a ring of some kind, which he drops into his pocket.

And so, the event that changes Middle-earth forever happens as easily as a small metal circle dropped into a wanderer's pocket. Eventually that ring will be used to destroy the greatest evil that has ever faced that world. Had Bilbo never been pulled from his comfortable living room, who knows what would've become of Middle-earth?

How many of your own positive developments and discoveries have come because you were taken to places you never wanted to go? Sometimes the universe has to drag us kicking and screaming to the things we will come to most treasure. It's almost enough to reaffirm one's faith that there really is a greater mind at work in the affairs of men and hobbits.

Certainly the Ring wanted to be rid of Gollum, so an evil will was at work. But it could've been picked up by a goblin or even some animal to transport it out of the caves. That it was found by a free hobbit whose heart was good was no accident.

It is at this point that Gollum enters our story. The Ring is his precious, but when he encounters Bilbo and wants to eat him, he still has no idea that the Ring has abandoned him.

Whether in fear or courage, or simple desperation, Bilbo draws his sword and brandishes it at Gollum. Again, it is fear that brings about heroism. How true that is, if heroism is there waiting to come out.

Gollum shows his own canniness by shifting from force to shrewdness, challenging Bilbo to a game of riddles—with the death or deliverance of Bilbo at stake.

But it is Bilbo's cleverness (though some would call it trickery) that gives him the victory. "What have I got in my pocket?" Gollum cannot guess, and so Bilbo has used his brain to prevail where his sword arm would probably not have.

When faced with fear or evil, a direct assault is not always the most prudent response. Often it is the right choice, however, and the failure to act with force when force is called for will lead only to more evil in the future. It takes wisdom to know whether sword or subtlety is called for against any given foe.

Despite Bilbo's victory, Gollum intends to eat him. He returns to his island to retrieve the Ring, which he will don to sneak up on Bilbo and vanquish him. But he realizes the Ring is lost, and he comes after Bilbo—now a true burglar, in Gollum's eyes, at least—to wrest it from him. But Bilbo "accidentally" puts the Ring on, turns invisible, and uses that power not only to find the way out of the caves but to escape the goblins guarding the entrance.

Bilbo may have entered these caves—the belly of the beast, in hero's journey terms—as an untried neophyte, but he emerges as a sly thinker who, in this case, at least, has mastered his fear enough to keep his head and use what advantages come to him in the heat of a crisis.

Consider Luke Skywalker in the bowels of the Death Star. He enters as a spoiled farm boy, but when he comes out on the other side of that trial, he is a hero capable of great deeds.

What crucible have you been through that made you a better person? By definition, a crucible is something painful and even destructive. Life turns up the heat beyond your ability to withstand it—and it transforms you from one state of being into another. It purifies you, allowing the junk to be swept away and the true value to pour out and form into something strong and fine. What crucibles have you been through?

In Bilbo's case, he not only learned how to use his mind to deal with fearful situations, he also found the key to, well, pretty much everything. Crucibles have been known to do that.

What beneficial lessons—or magical talismans, so to speak—have you learned, through duress, that you would never have found had you not been forced to endure it?

The next time you find yourself in a crisis, look not only for the smart way to handle it but also for the powerful key that might be sitting on the ground right beside you.

Heeding Warnings

Bilbo is reunited with Gandalf and the dwarves but is soon threatened again, this time by wargs who summon the goblins. The intrepid group is rescued by giant eagles who bear them to safety.

Sometimes our enemies team up against us, and sometimes help comes from unexpected places.

Gandalf leaves the group again (one might begin to suspect that some big trial is ahead of them...) but leaves them in the care of Beorn, a man-bear creature, who sends them on a secret path toward their destination. He warns them that the journey is dangerous and they must not depart from the path. But we know what they will do. They soon become separated in the dark forest of Mirkwood, and Bilbo wakes up and finds his legs bound with sticky filaments and a giant spider advancing on him.

The more perilous the task, the more careful one must be to attend to procedure. Anyone can start a fire in a forest, but it takes great care and training to maintain a helpful fire that clears away the underbrush but doesn't become an inferno. Anyone could attempt to rescue someone caught in raging floodwaters, but it takes extreme care to emerge from that struggle with a positive result. Having said that, the rewards of successfully navigating a tricky bit of water can be tremendous.

Had the dwarves and Bilbo followed directions precisely, had they simply stayed on the path, they would've come out from their forest journey unharmed and much nearer their destination. Instead, they ignored what they'd been told, and they nearly paid the ultimate price.

Has it been that way for you? Have you ever felt that the warnings you'd been given were too alarmist or legalistic, and should be discarded? Have you ever rejected someone's advice but ended up wishing you'd listened?

Some lessons can't be learned unless you go against what someone has told you to do. Has any child ever really believed his parent's warning that the stove top was very hot? Probably not many. And even though a child might believe that stuffing yourself with candy or cake will make you sick, she still has to try it at least once.

Not that this will prevent you from warning others not to touch the stove top or stuff themselves with sweets. We *should* warn them, even if we know they probably won't listen.

Naming Your Weapon

Back to Bilbo, who with bound legs is facing a monstrous spider. It's the stuff of nightmares.

But this is not the same Bilbo who left the Shire, even if he doesn't realize he has changed. This is a hobbit who has faced so many dire threats in such a short time that he's almost beginning to consider such things his normal way of being. So he whips out his short sword, cuts himself free, and slays the giant spider.

He can't quite believe it, and he even passes out for a bit. But when he awakens:

> The spider lay dead beside him, and his sword-blade was stained black. Somehow the killing of the giant spider, all alone by himself in the dark without the help of the wizard or the dwarves or of anyone else, made a great difference to Mr. Baggins. He felt a different person, and much fiercer and bolder in spite of an empty stomach, as he wiped his sword on the grass and put it back into its sheath. "I will give you a name," he said to it, "and I shall call you Sting." (*The Hobbit*, chapter 8)

This is the key moment in Bilbo's inner journey. Everything that came before was preparation for this instant, and everything that came after is the testing and using of this change, now that it has occurred.

Here Bilbo has become a man—or an adult hobbit, if you prefer. All alone, by himself, in the dark, and without the help of a powerful wizard or a band of hardy dwarves, Bilbo has slain a monster. Being small couldn't get him out of danger, nor would any riddle or trick deliver him. It came down to the strength of his arm and the edge of his sword.

And he was victorious.

Defining moments come according to a schedule we know nothing about. Perhaps it is a house suddenly afire or a revolution we become caught up in or a decision made by someone else that puts us in the front row of the decision of our lives. It doesn't matter how or when it comes. What matters is what we do when it's upon us.

We are all on an inner journey. We are all forced out of our Shires and cast into the belly of the beast. We all face fears and evils beyond our reckoning or power to escape. We all encounter enemies, and we all have to go through crucibles and learn things the hard way. Most crucially, we all come to our moment of truth, when everything else falls away, and it is only our choice that matters, and heaven and earth stand by to see what we will choose.

Have you had your moment yet? Chances are, you've at least had several smaller ones—little moments of truth that have each led to the next one. Eventually a moment will come that will forever shape your personality, either because you responded well in that moment and you like what you have become, or because you responded poorly and you vow to spend the rest of your life making up for it.

If you are past that moment, think back on it. Stop to ponder it before moving on.

The ancient biblical patriarchs used to erect piles of stones to mark where something significant happened. They wanted to always remember what had happened—and they wanted their children to ask what those piles of rocks were, so there would be opportunities to rehearse the story again.

Bilbo marked this event by giving his sword a name: Sting. Now it was no longer a knife, and he was no longer just a woebegotten hobbit. Now the sword was a powerful talisman, and he was a warrior to be reckoned with.

With the naming of Sting, Bilbo passed from the realm of childhood to the realm of adulthood. He was no longer a passive victim to whom terrible things happened. Now he was a doer of great deeds. The difference cannot be overemphasized.

Which are you?

While this moment marks the end of Bilbo's transformation, it is not the end of his hero's journey. The purpose of the journey is to create a hero—not for the mere sake of it, but in order that this individual can confront the great evil that is threatening the land.

From this point on in *The Hobbit*, Bilbo is a doer of heroic deeds. With his sword and his ring and his brain, he rescues the dwarves from the spiders, and then from the Wood-elves, and then from the dragon itself, and finally from the Battle of Five Armies. Had the dwarves not been given their reluctant burglar from Bag End, they would've perished ten times over and never reached, much less won, the object of their quest.

Are you a doer of great deeds? Are those in your care protected because you are in their lives? Slay your monster, name your sword, and take your place among the heroes.

Conclusion

Bilbo faced great fear and evil, and he emerged a hero. We could trace Frodo's journey just as well, for it follows the same path from childlike victim to responsible champion.

What have been the steps of your hero's journey? Where are you on that map? What might you do to advance to the next phase?

Should you take it, the journey will change you forever. You will never again be the innocent you once were. The fears faced and the responsibilities accepted transform you.

It is said that the person who returns home after going on his hero's journey will never need to go on it again. Instead he becomes the mentor, the wise wizard to a new generation of those just beginning the journey. If you have been on this journey—there and back again—who around you might benefit from what you have learned?

When Gandalf chose Bilbo to be the burglar for the dwarves, he said this to ease their misgivings: "There is a lot more in him than you guess, and a deal more than he has any idea of himself."

So it is with you.

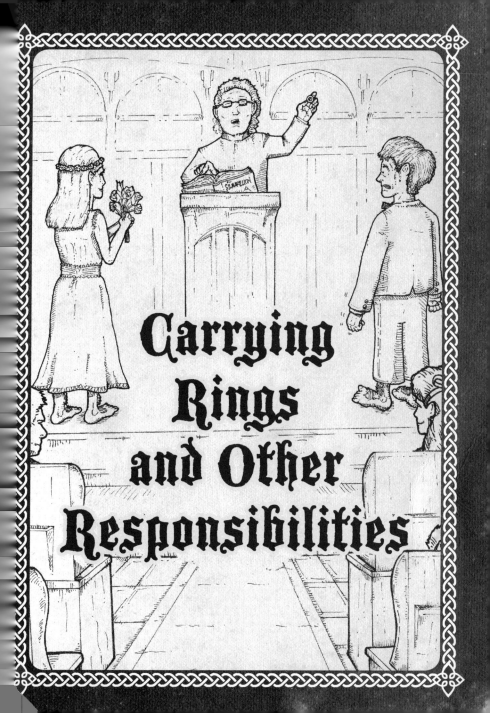

Carrying Rings and Other Responsibilities

Sam!" cried Frodo. "What have I said? What have I done? Forgive me! After all you have done. It is the horrible power of the Ring. I wish it had never, never, been found. But don't mind me, Sam. I must carry the burden to the end. It can't be altered. You can't come between me and this doom."

—Frodo in JRR Tolkien's
The Return of the King

When *The Hobbit* begins, Bilbo Baggins is a typical member of hobbit society.

> The Bagginses had lived in the neighbourhood of The Hill for time out of mind, and people considered them very respectable, not only because most of them were rich, but also because they never had any adventures or did anything unexpected; you could tell what a Baggins would say on any question without the bother of asking him.
> (*The Hobbit*, chapter 1)

Being among the hobbit aristocracy, as it were, Bilbo had certain obligations to maintain. If it's true he never did anything unexpected, then it means he did everything that was expected of him. Doubtless he took part in civic affairs when called upon, weighed in on matters of import, and took his turn in a variety of leadership posts over his long lifetime before he went on his unexpected journey.

But he had not always been like that. As with the rural Brits of the 1930s, upon whom Tolkien's hobbits were modeled, Bilbo and his contemporaries doubtless avoided responsibility for as long as possible, especially during the irresponsible tweens.

Even into adulthood, hobbit males preferred to fish or drink or smoke or eat—and preferably all in a single outing—rather than tend to crops or brush down the ponies or do anything else that resembled work. If the women of the Shire didn't catch them, even hobbit grandfathers and other worthies would sneak out for a little libation instead of sweating under the sun.

In short, Bilbo was a leading member of a group of reluctant workers always pining for the end of the workday, rather like school children. Responsibility might be thrust upon them, and indeed they might do well when forced to exercise it, but it was never their preference.

So how is it that Bilbo came to command the respect of battle-hardened dwarves, men, and elves? How is it that Frodo—a fine young hobbit if ever there was one—came to bear the weight of Middle-earth on his narrow shoulders? And what can we learn from their examples?

Let us see. (Note: This chapter is best read with Howard Shore's soundtrack to *The Hobbit* or *The Lord of the Rings* playing in the background. It's suitably thoughtful and even somber at times.)

Do What Must Be Done

All of us would rather play than work. Doing what we want is always preferable to doing what we must do. Even things that are themselves enjoyable—like art, playing a game, being at Disney World, or going on safari—can become tiresome and unpleasant if we're not careful.

How lucky are those who truly love what they do for a living? To wrap one's genuine joy into a job that provides a comfortable living, to love getting up in the morning and going to work, is the dream of pretty much every adult.

Someone in a job he or she doesn't entirely love needs to find something to love in that job. Maybe the work is mind-numbing, but your coworkers are interesting and worth investing time and attention in. Maybe the working conditions are less than desirable, but you're doing something that will benefit and perhaps even protect others. It could be that the office dynamics are somewhat dysfunctional, but the wage you're bringing home allows you and your family to take trips, thereby creating memories you will treasure.

Doing the thing you don't want to do, simply because it must be done, is being responsible.

Bilbo and his fellow hobbits knew this. Even the most irresponsible twentysomething hobbit male understood that if he wanted food, someone would have to prepare it—maybe even him. It wasn't by Gandalf's magic that the Green Dragon was supplied with meat and drink. Nor did Wood-elves sneak in at night and build the furniture or furnish the rooms or load the firewood. Rangers of the North might have guarded the borders of the Shire, but they weren't hunting, dressing, and cooking deer for the hobbits to eat.

Play is what a hobbit earned by his work. The idea that a person must contribute to the welfare of the group before he can partake of that group's bounty is not something we've invented in the age of men. You must eat your vegetables before you get your dessert. You must do the schoolwork before you get to play on the team or march in the band. You retire with a nice pension only after you have given your decades of faithful service.

Are there areas in your life where you might need to work a little harder? Have you let something important slide because it's more fun to go out and play? Or, are you working too long or too much and not giving yourself the fun you sorely need? If hobbits can be counted on for anything, it's to be examples of how to cut loose. Maybe you need to do a bit more of that yourself.

Play is vital to mental health, but we emulate the responsibility of a Bilbo or a Frodo when we defer our fun times until we have first accomplished what must be done.

Responsibility and Character

At the beginning of *The Hobbit*, Bilbo is timid, uncertain, and com- placent. He is passive. He does what is expected of him. Is it praise or condemnation when others say that he is so utterly non-noteworthy that his opinion is known without the need to ask it of him?

When he is whisked away with the dwarves as their untried bur- glar, he feels a correspondingly low sense of responsibility to the group. One wonders if he might even wish some calamity to come upon the dwarves that would allow him to scamper back to the Shire.

Sometimes we, too, are thrust into situations we did not choose. Selected for a task we didn't want, "volunteered" for an errand that will eat up our Saturday, stuck taking the neighbor kids with us to the boat show.

When that happens, it is natural to feel that we aren't responsible for what happens. It wasn't our choice to be doing this (or to be doing it in this way), so who cares how it turns out? Our feeling of involve- ment is low.

So when Bilbo scouted ahead and encountered three trolls eat- ing roast mutton, he did not go back and warn the dwarves. Wouldn't they have appreciated knowing "that there were three fair-sized trolls at hand in a nasty mood, quite likely to try toasted dwarf, or even pony, for a change"? Oh, he thought he probably should tell them, but he didn't.

When we feel put-upon to do something we don't want to do, it often takes a while for us to think responsibly about the people we're with or for whom we're doing such put-upon things. "It's not my car," or "They're not my kids."

They're not my dwarves.

Sometimes it takes calamity—or a near miss—to bring us to our senses and make us begin to care.

Bilbo watched the trolls capture all the dwarves except Thorin, and in the midst of this disaster, suddenly he engaged. He warns Thorin of the trolls, and when the dwarf began to fight the trolls, Bilbo actually dove in. Not that a hobbit holding on to a troll's ankle would do much in a scuffle, but we're looking at the size of his heart here, not the size of his body.

After the serendipitous return of Gandalf and the escape of their entire company, Bilbo was more—and permanently—engaged with the fate of the group. He volunteered the trolls' key that opened the door to their stash, which led to the discovery of magical swords that benefitted not only his dwarven companions but a mighty wizard.

As his own reward, Bilbo received a knife in a leather sheath, "only a tiny pocket-knife for a troll, but ... as good as a short sword for the hobbit." In due time, others would feel the sting of this knife.

And it all came about because Bilbo went from not caring for the people he was with to throwing in with them. And with every adventure he would face with them, though the adventures became increasingly difficult and dangerous, Bilbo accepts more and more responsibility for the safety of the group and its mission.

Our own character is tested when we are put into situations against our will. Our resentment at being overruled may express itself in a lack of concern for the outcome of the effort or the welfare of those we're forced to be around.

That's natural (human, even) and isn't really the issue. What matters is how we respond as the situation proceeds. Riding that nonchalance and disconnection for a long time reveals a lack of nobility in our character.

What reveals good character is when we decide that, even though we didn't choose this development, we're going to behave as moral, responsible people nonetheless.

When we do, who knows what rewards will come our way. Maybe they will come in the form of wealth or powerful new tools, or maybe it will just be the richness we receive when we honestly invest in the lives of those around us.

Use Your Rings Wisely

Wouldn't it be nice to have a magic ring? Keeping in mind Gandalf's warning that "There are many magic rings in this world, Bilbo Baggins, and none of them should be used lightly," it would still be pretty amazing to have one.

Poor Frodo had almost none of the "fun" of having such a ring, but he had more than his share of the danger. It would be better to have been Bilbo back in the time when Sauron was just the Necromancer in Mirkwood and hadn't the strength or the knowledge to come looking for the Ring in the Shire.

Bilbo could put that ring on whenever he felt like it. He'd vanish and a whole new realm of possibilities opened up to him.

Invisibility

What would you do with a ring that made you invisible? Spy on someone? Sneak away from obnoxious Sackville-Bagginses? Approach villains unaware and deal with them like a superhero? Shoplift? Leave anonymous gifts? Gain access to restricted areas?

A magical ring, like any great boon, reveals what is inside the bearer's heart. Being given one is akin to being asked, "What would you do if you could do anything and get away with it scot-free?"

Bilbo's ring, like the nine rings given to the great men of old, made the wearer invisible and granted long life. It wasn't until the One Ring passed to Frodo that its power to corrupt became evident. But even without Sauron's influence tugging toward evil, a magical ring would have the tendency to lead the wearer in the wrong direction.

How much of what we do—and don't do—is determined by the fact that someone might catch us doing it? If you remove that accountability and give someone absolute anonymity, what might he or she become capable of?

The old saying, "Character is who you are when no one is looking," takes on new significance when we're talking about rings of invisibility.

But even without a magical ring, modern technology gives each one of us stealth capability, especially when dealing with people on the Internet. Give someone a username that masks his identity, set him loose among other people who may or may not be who they show themselves to be, and all manner of normally forbidden behavior becomes possible.

Spend an hour on an online multiplayer game, and you'll see people using language and talking about topics that would make their friends and family gasp. Most likely, these gamers would never say such things when someone could hear them and identify them as the speaker. But grant invisibility, and who knows what will crawl out of his heart?

There have been many examples in the news of sexual predators using online chatrooms and Facebook to lure new victims. They give themselves harmless-sounding names—names that make them seem like another child, for instance—and start their stalking.

Bilbo showed remarkable character and restraint while using his ring. He put it on to save his friends or sneak into dungeons to effect their release. If the power of anonymity reveals what is in a person's heart, then what was in Bilbo's heart was great indeed. When you have power to help or harm and you choose to help, you are shown to be noble.

Faramir, Captain of Gondor, had such power over Frodo and Sam. When it came time for him to show his worth, he chose to help, not harm, though it might have cost him his very life. His character, as Sam says, is the very finest.

Do you have power to do good or evil to someone? Are you unwatched in certain situations, giving you opportunity to harm or help, protect or pilfer? If so, when it is time for you to show your worth, what will you do?

Very Long Life

The One Ring and the nine given to men gave not only invisibility but also long life.

What would you do with three lifetimes?

The elves never died of old age. They might be killed in battle or through some accident, but never due to advanced age. They spent their long lives honoring their traditions, making music and making skillful crafts, preserving their lands, and at times allying with others against evil.

In the *Highlander* series of movies and shows, certain characters were immortal. Unless they were killed by beheading, they lived endlessly.

Can you imagine living so long? You wouldn't have to worry about dying before some project was finished or some person had come of age. You wouldn't be bothered if something took "forever" to accomplish.

Would you make friends with those living a normal lifespan? Would it break your heart to marry and have children if you knew you would watch them grow old and die while you simply lingered? Would you prefer to be isolated?

What views would you hold if you were going to live indefinitely? What chances would you take if you knew you would survive virtually any mishap? How would you view fads and trends if you'd seen millions of them come and go over your lifetime?

What would a responsible life look like if it were measured in centuries instead of years?

We gain wisdom the older we get. That's a nice way of saying that we make a lot of mistakes in this life. Hopefully we learn from them, at least enough so we don't make them again. We may not have a magical ring giving us unnaturally long life, but the chances are good that there are people around us who could benefit from our hard-earned wisdom.

Who in your circle of friends and family might be helped by what you have to offer? You can't come across as a know-it-all, of course, or no one will pay heed. But can you think of people or groups you could talk to who might find your knowledge useful? One person held back from making a bad decision because of what you said would be considered a victory.

Give someone the benefit of the lessons you've learned, whether you've learned them over many lifetimes or just one.

The Pull of Evil

Magic rings, like great wealth or unchecked power, can lead the owner either to good or to evil. As we have seen, such things reveal what is in the bearer's heart.

How many lottery winners end up in misery? Some descend into depression. Many wind up in poverty. And some even commit suicide. How can this be? Surely having unlimited wealth thrust upon a man would make him happy.

That's not to say that there aren't very wealthy people who live full lives in joy and contentment, because there certainly are many people like that.

The point is that great wealth or power can change a person. Whatever things were kept repressed in a person's heart when he did not have that wealth or power are now set loose. If you didn't do something magnanimous because you lacked the money to do it, suddenly the option is back on the table. If you didn't do something that perhaps the culture would frown upon, you might have kept it inside for fear of losing your job if it went wrong. But with no fear of losing your economic plenty, such things might occur to you again.

We are forever pulled in good directions and bad. Most of us are simultaneously blessed and cursed with the inability to follow those directions to any extreme. But with great power and wealth comes great freedom to do what might previously have been impossible.

The One Ring gave invisibility, enhanced hearing, and prolonged life. It gave vision into a previously hidden realm of existence. It gave a portion of power relative to the bearer's strength of will. But it also exerted a malicious influence that tugged its bearer always toward darkness.

Even Gandalf and Galadriel, two of the most powerful beings in Middle-earth, would not be able to avoid the corrupting power of the Ring forever. If such paragons of character could not resist that downward slide, how could a typical person?

In one major respect at least, wealth and power are unlike the power of the Ring: Wealth and power are neutral. They have no inherent moral bent toward good or evil. They are revealers, not destroyers, of character.

In what areas are you inclined toward light or darkness? In what ways are you being tugged toward one or the other but feel you don't have the ability to act now? This isn't an encouragement to commit a crime or infidelity. This is simply an invitation to reflect on what is inside you at the moment. If you suddenly had unlimited wealth or power, would you do those things?

Maybe you can't bequeath millions to your favorite charity or to build a playground or to have the hospital add that special wing you'd like to see. But who says you can't do something small right now? Maybe you could buy a commemorative brick in the hospital's building campaign or even volunteer there on Saturdays. It has been suggested that what we do with little is representative of what we would do with much. So why not go ahead and pitch your "little" toward the good you wish you could do more for?

Now about those rings that tend toward evil: Do you have anything in your life that is pulling you in the wrong direction? Anything—or anyone—bringing out the dark side in you?

Consider the seven rings given to dwarves. They didn't extend life or bestow invisibility. In fact, their only known power was to awaken avarice and anger.

Can you imagine owning something that actually caused you to be angry? Or wearing something that automatically caused your greed to soar? It's hard to imagine how this would be seen as a boon to anyone. But perhaps the dwarves used the power to amass wealth, thinking they could take the rings off whenever they chose.

Many religious traditions teach that both good and evil want to have our allegiance, that both are at work inside us vying for control. In such a situation, if there were talismans that pulled us toward one or the other, it seems we would want them. We'd want the ring that pulled us toward good, if good was what we desired; and we'd want the ring that encouraged our negative attributes, if we wanted to give ourselves over to evil.

But we'd certainly not want the object that pulled us in the direction we did not want to go.

What (or who) do you have in your life that is causing you to move in the wrong direction?

Letting Go of Rings

The One Ring had a will of its own. It chose the bearer who could get it back to its evil master. If a bearer didn't take it in the right direction, the Ring would abandon it in an attempt to "trade up," to find a new bearer who would more perfectly obey its will.

When the Ring was done with you, it would slip off and betray you. You'd be rid of it whether you wanted to be or not. And most likely you wouldn't want to be rid of it.

But if the Ring is not finished with you, you would certainly not want it to be parted from you.

Some negative influences in our lives are just like that. We know we should distance ourselves from that place or person or activity or web page or group or realm of activity, and indeed we mean to. But somehow we find it in our pocketses.

The Ring never had its wearer's good at heart, unless its wearer was Sauron. Similarly, those negative influences just mentioned are not looking out for your best interests. Their end is destruction.

So how do you let go of something that is hurting you or those around you, but that doesn't want to let go of you?

First, you should do all you can to remove yourself from the thing that is causing you to do (or to be tempted to do) evil. It is not unwise to simply stop watching that show or listening to that commentator or chatting with that friend if, afterward, you are left in a worse place than when you began.

Sometimes we can't just do that. Perhaps it's a toxic relationship that requires a more careful treatment than simply walking away. Perhaps it's part of our workplace or family. Or perhaps its claws are in us too deeply for us to step away using only our own power.

In that case, we might need the help of someone else. As Frodo discovered at the Cracks of Doom, even an enemy can do the dearest work of friendship when you're too far gone. Had Gollum not bitten the Ring off Frodo's hand, what would have become of Middle-earth?

Those around you can help you be rid of the "ring" that is drawing you toward destruction. Maybe it's a friend or a spouse or a parent. Maybe it's a co-worker or a counselor or a clergyman. And maybe it's a group or organization or clinic.

Fortunate is the one who has a friend to pick him up when he stumbles. Pity the man one who has no one to catch him when he falls.

It's possible, of course, to defy even the best intervention. Perhaps the wound is so deep or the addiction so strong that even professional help isn't enough. Sometimes we have to be saved from ourselves.

Happily, as Gandalf reminded another Ringbearer, we're not in this alone: "There are other forces at work in this world, Frodo, besides the will of evil."

Frodo was carried along by more than the Fellowship and the goodwill of all the Free Peoples of Middle-earth.

So are we all. Whether you cry out to the Universe, God, the Force, or a Higher Power, you probably do cry out to someone or something. It is the natural human condition to have faith in some being greater than man. Atheism must be learned.

If you have a "ring" that you just can't seem to let go of, admit it and call out for rescue.

Sometimes help comes in the form of disappointment or failure. A certain man had gone to seminary and was hoping to become a hospital chaplain at a pediatric hospital. But try as he might, he couldn't find a chaplaincy program that would accept him. It caused him deep despair, as he felt he could happily spend his entire career as a hospital chaplain, if only he could find a position.

When his failures continued to mount, he finally took a job in an entirely different field—and he is immensely happy he did. He never would've been able to make it as a chaplain, he now realizes.

Sometimes it is a blessing not to get what you want.

If you have a ring that is pulling you toward evil but that you can't get away from, no matter how hard you try, call out to those higher powers to bring the break. And if there is something you can't achieve no matter how hard you try, perhaps that is your signal to try harder and without ceasing because it is the direction you should go. But there's also the possibility that it is another force at work in your life blocking you from this, not to frustrate you but to bring about your better outcome.

Some rings must be let go of or they could send you plunging into the Cracks of Doom.

Conclusion

Hobbits, or the males of the species, at any rate, are not by nature responsible creatures. If a magic ring came to them, it would most likely bend their wills to its own mind.

For a while, having a magic ring would be good fun. It would allow the hobbit to blink out of view when unpleasant relatives were hanging on the bell, and it would no doubt result in many vegetarian delights to be lifted from right under Farmer Maggot's nose.

But eventually the ring would begin its downward pull. It is the rare hobbit—or man, for that matter—who would lift himself to the challenge of doing not what is fun to do but what must be done.

Ordinary people, too, have responsibilities that must be tended to, though a party would be much more fun. Happily, we have more Frodo in us than we might realize. It is very good that this ring of responsibility has come to us, because we will bear it for as long as it is ours to carry.

Praps ye sits here and chats with it a bitsy, my preciousss. It likes riddles, praps it does, does it?"

—Gollum, from JRR Tolkien's
The Hobbit

Hobbits are very skilled at riddles—much more so than, say, men or dwarves (or even elves). Being close to the earth, they understand its humor, and riddles are born of the earth.

Mr. Baggins, a pretty average hobbit (perhaps a little smarter and a little more courageous than most, though he doesn't yet know it), is ready to take on the mysterious Gollum at riddling games. In fact, he even dares to think that he might beat the slimy creature. After all, hobbits spend a great deal of time sitting by the fire in the winter months making up and guessing at riddles. They've even come up with some questions that are remarkably difficult for other inhabitants of Middle-earth to guess.

If you're confronted by riddles, here are some hints about how to approach them.

- **RIDDLES ARE ALL ABOUT MISDIRECTION.** The solutions are always obvious and standing in plain sight.
- **RIDDLES ARE ABOUT WORD PLAY.** Hobbits are fascinated by words—this is a sign of their connection to elves. The more you enjoy riddles and word games, the more elvish you are.
- **RIDDLES ARE ANCIENT.** Bilbo himself knows that even a very old creature such as Gollum is going to know the basic rules of riddling.
- **RIDDLES ARE A KEY TO GREATER TRUTH.** In fact, the adventures of Bilbo, and later of Frodo, are a great riddle, and one to which the answer ultimately lies in the Undying West.

Who Likes Riddles?

It's quite possible you may come into situations in which riddles are the most reasonable response to a given challenge. If so, you might ask what kind of people (or creatures) are riddling you. Their reaction to riddles will probably reveal something about their personalities, too.

Elves and Riddles

Elves, on the whole, like riddles. Which is to say, they like random, nonresponsive, confusing answers to questions. Frodo comments to Gildor, "It is said, Go not to the Elves for counsel, for they will say both no and yes." The elf admits the justice of this remark. Elrond also has a habit of making cryptic comments that don't make much sense—unless you're a half-elf or a wizard. And Galadriel is positively Delphic in most of her utterances while the Fellowship is vacationing in Lothlórien. All in all, the elves like a style of communication that is confusing, cryptic, and only understandable by other elves. This makes them highly susceptible to riddles and other guessing games.

The only problem with starting a riddling contest with an elf is that it's likely to go on for days, as the riddles get more and more obscure, bound up in lore that's thousands of years old and remembered only by the elves, and even then not many of them. So don't start riddling with elves unless you have plenty of time on your hands and nothing urgent in the offing (such as saving Middle-earth from the Dark Lord by dropping his ring in a volcano).

Dwarves and Riddles

Dwarves are plain, down-to-Middle-earth folk with no time for nonsense—riddling or anything else. Dwarf lore is largely a matter of transmitting plain, ordinary fact, although every now and then there's a bit of mysticism wrapped up in it, such as the Mirrormere and the myths surrounding Khazad-dûm. But who wants to spend his time speculating on the answers to obscure questions when there's ale to be drunk, beards to be grown, and orcs to be slain?

If you want to start a riddling contest with a dwarf, be sure to make the stakes worth his while: a pile of gold coins, perhaps, or a trinket or two made of *mithril*; possibly a couple of barrels of well-brewed ale to go along with a nice stash of Longbottom Leaf (since dwarves are notorious connoisseurs of pipeweed).

Men and Riddles

Let's face it: Compared to most other races of Middle-earth, men are a bit simpleminded. (The exception is Númenóreans, but there aren't many of them around. We're talking about normal, average, everyday men.) They aren't nearly as mystic and complex as the elves, and they don't have strong connections to the earth like dwarves do. However, they generally like riddling speech, as witness the strange dream that Faramir and then, once, Boromir have:

> Seek for the Sword That Was Broken
> In Imladris It Dwells
> There shall be counsels taken
> Stronger than Morgul Spells

And so on.

In point of fact, men rather like riddles, since riddles are mysterious and allow for days—months, sometimes—of endless debate, thus shutting off any need to take action.

From this point of view, the best time to start a riddling contest with a man is when he's contemplating some disastrous course of action and you want to delay him as long as possible from making an ass of himself and possibly bringing ruin on everyone else. Gods sometimes come down from the heavens to challenge mortal men to riddling contests as a way of testing man's wisdom and deciding if they're truly worthy of ruling.

Orcs and Riddles

Orcs don't like riddles. They don't like anything confusing. All
they want is to get a plain answer to plain questions, preferably
with a little torture to go with it, and then get on with slaughtering and rampaging. If you're stuck in a dungeon with a couple of
grumpy orcs, don't try to riddle them. Spend your mental energy
thinking of a way to escape with most of your skin intact.

Dragons and Riddles

Dragons like riddles. They're fascinated by riddling speech, as witness Smaug's reaction when Bilbo tells riddles during their conversation. There's a lot of riddling talk, and Smaug loves it—which is
why he doesn't end the conversation right then and there by blowing
Bilbo to ashes with his fiery breath. The rules here, if you're talking to
dragons, are:

- **KEEP THE TOPICS LIGHT.** Don't spend any time on famous elvish warriors who've slain dragons or notable dwarves who've
  been able to defeat the great Wyrms of the North. Instead, stay
  on topics such as the weather, food, and what the well-dressed
  dragon is wearing this season.

- **REMEMBER THAT DRAGONS ARE SENSITIVE TO THE SUBJECT
  OF WEALTH (ESPECIALLY THEIR OWN).** Dragons have spent a
  good deal of time accumulating their hoards, so it's very rude
  to suggest that anyone else might have a claim to them.

- **GIVE THE DRAGON AN OPPORTUNITY TO SHOW OFF ITS JEWEL-
  ENCRUSTED UNDERBELLY BY TELLING IT HOW MAGNIFICENT IT
  IS.** Dragons like to boast as much as the next magical beast.
  They also appreciate fulsome praise. Who knows? You may
  discover something useful.

- **TRY NOT TO BRING UP PAST HEROES WHO MAY HAVE
  CHALLENGED THEM AND WHOSE DESCENDANTS ARE STILL
  AROUND, POSING A DISTANT, BUT NONETHELESS DISTINCT
  THREAT.** Dragons, like other magical beasts, have extremely
  long memories.

- **DON'T SHOPLIFT HIS TREASURE.** For goodness sakes, this is just plain manners! How'd you like it if someone came into your house and stole the teaspoons? Just because a big two-handled goblet is lying there in plain sight is no reason to take it.

Hobbits

Hobbits love riddles and have a rich store of them. Except for one or two instances, Bilbo really isn't at a loss for a riddle when Gollum presses him—except for the very end of the game when he rather unfairly demands to know, "What have I got in my pockets?" Experts and authorities have quite reasonably pointed out that this isn't a riddle and therefore, by the strict rules of the game, Bilbo has lost. However, when he accepts the challenge to guess the answer to the hobbit's question, Gollum implicitly also accepts the new rules and obligates himself to abide by the result. Of course he's not going to. It's just that from a strictly moral standpoint, he ought to.

If you challenge a hobbit to a riddle game, and the hobbit is stuck for a riddle (by which right, he ought to surrender the game), don't give in if he starts asking irrelevant questions like "What have I got in my pockets?" or "What was the first name of my aunt's mother's grandmother's second cousin?" If he can't think of a true riddle, inform the hobbit that he's lost; it's as simple as that.

What Makes a Good Riddle?

Some riddles are based on word play; others are about what you don't know. Bilbo is skilled at both. Others prove themselves somewhat less adept. Tolkien's stories are filled with riddles, and it would make things easier for many of the characters if they could answer them earlier and more correctly.

Boromir's Riddle

When he comes to the Council of Elrond, Boromir of Gondor tells the assembled elves, dwarves, hobbits, and men of a riddle that his brother, Faramir, heard in a dream:

> See for the sword that was broken
> In Imladris it dwells.
> There shall be counsels taken
> Stronger than Morgul spells.
> There shall be shown a token
> That doom is near at hand.
> For Isildur's Bane shall waken
> And the Halfling forth shall stand.

On the surface, this is pretty clear, especially when it's all explained to Boromir at the council. Yet he persists in misunderstanding bits of it, even when Tolkien practically hits him over the head with it. The same thing is true of Faramir when, later in the story, he actually meets Frodo and Samwise and learns of the Ring. We can only see Boromir's failure to understand his riddle as a sign of the degeneration of the races of men and the evil that gnaws at the heart of Gondor. The lesson: When a bunch of elves, dwarves, hobbits, and men tell you something's true—believe it.

Aragorn's Riddle

When Bilbo first meets Aragon and the Ranger tells him his story, the hobbit is kind enough to make up a poem for the future king of Gondor in the form of riddling verse:

> All that is gold does not glitter.
> Not all those who wander are lost.
> The old that is strong does not wither.
> Deep roots are not touched by the frost.
> From the ashes a fire shall be woken.
> A light from the shadows shall spring.

Renewed shall be blade that was broken.
The crownless again shall be king.

You can't help feel that this is yet another example of hobbits and elves making things more difficult than they need to. If everyone knows Aragorn is the rightful king of Gondor, why not just say so? Surely it would make his claim to the throne stronger and make it harder for people such as Denethor to dispute the claim. Well, that's elves and hobbits for you. Always mixing things up in riddle-speak.

The Riddle of the Dead

At a key moment in the War of the Ring, Aragorn and the Grey Company make a fateful decision: They will ride to the Stone of Erech and pass through the kingdom of the dead. At this point, the sons of Elrond bring a message from their father: "Bid Aragorn remember the words of the seer, and remember the paths of the dead."

Not terribly encouraging words, on the whole, but the Ranger remembers (because he's wise in the lore of Middle-earth) the words spoken by Malbeth the Seer:

Over the land there lies a long shadow,
Westward reaching wings of darkness
The Tower trembles; to the tombs of kings
Doom approaches. The Dead awaken
For the hour is come for the oathbreakers:
At the Stone of Erech they shall stand again.

"Dark ways, doubtless," Gimli the dwarf remarks sourly, "but not darker than these staves are to me." We can sympathize with the dwarf. After all, remember, dwarves like plain speech better than riddling talk, and these comments of the Seer are confusing at best. However, Aragorn, true heir of kings, understands them and takes them as an indication that at this dark hour he should ride the paths of the dead.

The lesson here is when you don't have any better road, follow the riddle. Because, awful as its advice may be, it's probably better than the alternative.

Riddles in the Dark

The most famous riddling contest in history is unquestionably when Bilbo meets Gollum deep in the bowels of the Misty Mountains. Neither is entirely sure of the other; each has something to gain from the other. And Bilbo has little choice but to play the game out to the end. We can all learn something from his selection of riddles.

What Has Roots as Nobody Sees

Gollum's first riddle describes something

> Taller than trees
> Up, up it goes
> And yet never grows.

A logical choice, since that's where he lives. What's more surprising is that Bilbo gets it right so quickly. "Easy, " he says. "Mountain, I suppose." In fact, there's nothing easy about it, since Bilbo comes from the gently rolling lands of the Shire, has never seen a mountain, and mistakes his first sight of the Misty Mountains for the Lonely Mountain, home of Smaug.

Thirty White Horses

Next Bilbo presents Gollum with his first riddle:

> Thirty white horses on a red hill,
> First they champ,
> Then they stamp,
> Then they stand still.

Well, if Gollum (as he tells Bilbo) "only has six," how does he know this chestnut's answer is "teeth"? Perhaps he's heard of other creatures who have more teeth than he does. Good advice for us, to be aware that riddles are meant to stir our minds and make us think outside our usual confines.

Wind and Sun

The next two riddles in the contest are about elemental forces, neither of which is especially liked by the contestant at whom it's directed. Gollum asks Bilbo about something that

> Wingless flutters,
> Toothless bites,
> Mouthless mutters

And it takes Bilbo a few minutes to think of the answer: "Wind. Wind, of course." He answers with a riddle that calls up images Gollum finds distasteful—making the point that if you're ever stuck in a tight place, find something that your opponent likes much worse.

An Eye in a Blue Face

Gollum is used to living underground, so Bilbo naturally thinks something along these lines will fool him:

> An eye in a blue face
> Saw an eye in a green face.
> "That eye is like to this eye"
> Said the first eye.

The answer—sun on daisies—upsets Gollum not so much for what it is than for the memories it evokes. It recalls distant days by the River when he used to go fishing with his cousin, Deagol. And, naturally, it causes him to make a mistake with his next riddle:

> It cannot be seen, cannot be felt,
> Cannot be heard, cannot be smelt.

Well, the answer's obvious, isn't it? Dark.

Fish and Eggs

There's nothing so obvious as that which you see every day. Bilbo thinks his riddle is dreadfully easy:

> A box without hinges, key, or lid,
> Yet golden treasure inside is hid

However, it puzzles Gollum for a good long time. He finally hisses the answer: eggs. The creature's reply is equally simple:

> Alive without breath, as cold as death,
> Never thirsty, ever drinking,
> All in mail, never clinking

But the hobbit is stumped, and he frantically turns over in his mind all the awful creatures who could be "cold as death." At the last second the answer—fish—comes to him. The lesson: It's the obvious things that are the most difficult.

Time, Time, Time

What could be more puzzling than something that conquers everything. Gollum asks,

> This thing all things devours;
> Birds, beast, trees, flowers;
> Gnaws iron, bites steel;
> Grinds hard stones to meal.

Of course, there's only one answer: Time. So when you're out of luck and out of everything else—you're never out of time.

What Has Bilbo Got in His Pocketses?

At the beginning of *The Lord of the Rings*, the author (in this case, presumably Frodo) observes, "The Authorities, it is true differ whether this last question (What have I got in my pockets) was a mere 'question' and not a 'riddle' according to the strict rule of the Game," but everyone agrees that Gollum, having agreed to the rules, was bound to answer. The biggest question, of course, was who the "authorities" were. After all, who really decides what's a riddle and what isn't? It turns out that riddling has some pretty specific rules.

If You're Going to Riddle, Know the Answers

Both Bilbo and Gollum know the answers to all the riddles they ask. That's better than the folks of Gondor, for example. Aragorn recites the words of Malbeth the Seer:

> Over the land there lies a long shadow
> Westward reaching wings of darkness.
> The Tower trembles to the tomb of kings
> Doom approaches; the Dead awaken.

He really has no idea what it means. Still, he knows, the best thing a king can do sometimes is to ride forward without question. So if you encounter a riddle to which you don't know the answer, trust in fate and ride forward blindly. Maybe things will work out all right after all.

The Answer to a Riddle Should Make Sense

Doubtless you've listened to riddles, puzzled over them, and when the answer was given, thought, *Well, of course! Why didn't I think of that?*

Some people, though, when riddling, keep the answers obscure or provide the answers in another language—Norwegian, or something.

> What's the name of the horse I saw you with last night?
> Svensk!

This goes beyond cheating; it's just irritating, and if you do this sort of thing to a dragon or a goblin, it'll probably be the last riddle you tell.

Riddles Should Come at Appropriate Times, Or, Never Laugh at Live Dragons

Asking riddles when you're cold, lost, and sitting on the edge of a dark lake, far underground, next to a slimy creature who has expressed a desire to eat you may not seem like the best time for a guessing game, but at least such a game would gain you some time to come up with a plan. The same is true when talking to a dragon. Dragons are fascinated by riddling talk, and you can keep them guessing as long as you keep your whereabouts concealed. However, when running down a narrow tunnel with an annoyed fire-breathing dragon behind you, it's not the best time to throw riddles, insults, or anything else. Just concentrate on running fast. Really, really fast.

Short Riddles Are Usually Harder to Solve Than Long Ones

It's notable that both Bilbo and Gollum ask short questions (in Bilbo's case, the egg riddle, and for Gollum the fish riddle) that turn out to be dreadfully hard to figure out. That's because short riddles give the guesser less to work with and more scope for confusion. Also remember that what's obvious to you is usually not so clear for someone else. So the clue in constructing a successful riddle may lie in focusing on your everyday experiences rather than the strange or exotic.

Other Famous Riddles

If you're stuck for a riddle, you might consider borrowing from riddles made famous by other great figures of history and legend. One of these is King Oedipus (better known, of course, for killing his father, marrying his mother, and giving us the Oedipus complex). As a young man, Oedipus confronted the Sphinx, the monster with the body of a lion and the head of a beautiful maiden. The Sphinx was accustomed to ask travelers a riddle; those who couldn't answer correctly (which up to that point, had been everybody) she killed and devoured. In its traditional form, the riddle of the Sphinx goes:

> It goes first on four legs in the morning
> Then on two legs in the afternoon
> Last on three legs in the evening

The answer, of course, is man, who crawls when a baby, walks on two legs in the prime of his life, and when he's old has to make use of a stick. Oedipus guessed the answer correctly, whereupon the Sphinx, taking defeat very hard, killed itself, and Oedipus became king of Thebes.

Alternate Versions

Another version of the Riddle of the Sphinx (and one that pays a greater tribute to Oedipus's ingenuity in coming up with the correct answer) runs like this:

> Two legs sat upon three legs
> With one leg in his lap;
> In comes four legs
> And runs away with one leg;
> Up jumps two legs,
> Catches up three legs,
> Throws it after four legs,
> And makes him bring one leg back.

The answer is a man sits on a stool, his stick on his lap. A dog comes in and steals the stick, whereupon the man grabs the stool and throws it at the dog, forcing the animal to return the stick.

Still another version of the Sphinx's riddle is:

> Two sisters
> One gives birth to the other
> She gives birth to the first

The answer is night and day.

Heidrek the Wise

In the Norse saga of King Heidrek the Wise, the god Odin, disguised as usual, shows up at Heidrek's court to challenge the king to a riddling contest. Finally Odin asks:

> What lives on high fells?
> What falls in deep dales?
> What lives without breath?
> What is never silent?
> This riddle ponder,
> O prince Heidrek

Heidrek, living up to his name, answers that "The raven lives ever on the high fells, the dew falls ever in the deep dells, the fish lives without breath, and the rushing waterfall is never silent." After this bit of wordplay, Odin has to concede that Heidrek is, indeed, wise.

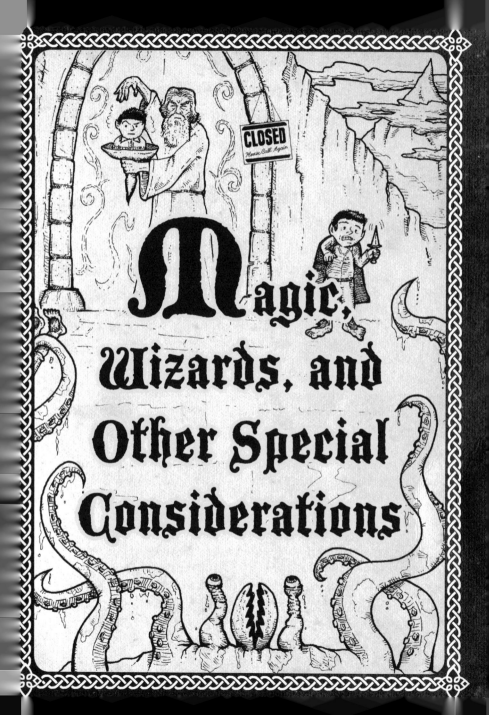

Magic, Wizards, and Other Special Considerations

or this is what your folk would call magic,
I believe; though I do not understand
clearly what they mean; and they seem
to use the same word of the deceits of
the Enemy. But this, if you will, is the
magic of Galadriel."

—Galadriel in JRR Tolkien's
The Fellowship of the Ring

Curiously, for anyone who visits Middle-earth for the first time, there doesn't seem to be a great deal of magic on display. Gandalf, it's true, employs fireworks (both as entertainment and as practical magic, when he's lighting a fire in the middle of a snowstorm far up on a mountainside in the Misty Mountains), but for the most part there's little magic readily available. Consider:

- When Glóin and Óin light a fire in *The Hobbit*, they use flint and steel, not magic.
- When Elrond reads the Moon Letters on the map of the Lonely Mountain possessed by Thorin, he uses ordinary skill (which, apparently, neither Thorin nor Gandalf possess, since they're both astonished that the map has Moon Runes).
- Hobbits are not in possession of magic, save "the ordinary everyday sort" that allows them to escape the notice of most of the creatures of Middle-earth. Bilbo is quite astonished at Gandalf's abilities to produce fire at a moment's notice.
- The elves of Mirkwood are apparently unable to conjure sufficient magic to guard their gates against escaping hobbits or

to at least detect invisible burglars in their midst. With such loose security protocols, you'd think they'd have long ago been invaded by goblins ... or something worse.

- Even Smaug—as magical a creature as it's possible to conceive—seems curiously lacking in magic. He relies on his fiery breath, his claws, and his great size to impose fear. The Lakemen, on the other hand, have the ability to speak with birds, which gives Bard the clue to the dragon's critical weakness.

When Guarding Against Magic

Never Mind About Counterspells

When Gandalf, challenged by the balrog in the depths of Moria, tries to put a counterspell on a door, the balrog replies with a counterspell that is so powerful it bursts the door and brings down the roof of the cavern. Gandalf assumes—mistakenly, it turns out—that the creature has buried itself and its supporting force of orcs. In fact, the logical conclusion of this episode is: Don't bother with counterspells when you're confronted with powerful magic. Just run. Fast. Away.

Know What Sort of Magic You're Dealing With

Middle-earth displays various kinds of magic. Some of it's benevolent (say, Gandalf's fireworks, used to entertain hobbits); some of it's weird but on the whole, good (Galadriel's mirror, which freaks out Samwise but otherwise is okay); and some of it's downright awful. For example, when the Fellowship is stranded in the Misty Mountains in the middle of a raging snowstorm, Boromir speculates that this may possibly be the work of Sauron.

"His arm has grown indeed," remarks Gimli, " if he can draw snow down from the North to trouble us here three hundred leagues away."

"His arm has grown long," replies Gandalf.

Don't Be Frightened By Magic

Some magic is scary (such as that employed by the Dark Lord) and
some of it is just strange. But some of it is, well, a bit out of the ordinary. For example, when the hobbits Frodo, Sam, Merry, and Pippin
are staying with Tom Bombadil, they're exposed to several different
kinds of magic, all of it relatively good.

- There's good magic when Tom chastises Old Man Willow
  and makes the troublesome tree release Merry and Pippin
  from its grip.
- There's weird magic, when Tom makes clear that the Ring of
  Power has no power over him.
- There's powerful magic, when Tom forces the barrow wight to
  release the four hobbits and breaks the spell of the barrow.

The rule to be derived from such encounters is this: Magic comes in
all shapes and sizes. Don't be overly concerned by the form it takes.
Just pay attention to what it does.

How to Call on Magic

It's best to start by recalling Gildor's words to Frodo: "Do not meddle
in the affairs of wizards, for they are subtle and quick to anger." Wizards are the beings of Middle-earth who have the right and the ability
to use magic on a daily basis, although there are some others—elves,
Dunedain, select dwarves—who take it upon themselves to try. The
basic point here is, don't use what you don't understand. If you don't
know the words of a spell, don't try to fake it. Elbereth knows what
you'll accidentally call up!

Magic Is All Around Us

Magic, as anyone in Middle-earth can tell you, isn't usually a matter of spells and incantations. It's more a matter of proper appreciation of what you have to work with. Take the Lady Galadriel: When
she works "magic" for Sam and Frodo with her mirror, all she does

is pour some water in a bowl, breathe on it, and tell them to look. That's hardly an impressive display of incantational powers. (Of course, it works, and, as is usual in such situations, they see much more than they intend to.)

The Proper Use of Palantiri

"Seeing stones" or palantiri are among the most powerful magical artifacts left by the ancient elves and others. Fëanor created the seeing stones in the distant depths of time, and even wizards are somewhat frightened of them. The palantiri in existence during the War of the Ring were:

- **THE SEEING STONE OF MORDOR.** Controlled by Sauron, this stone could see the other stones and could control, to some extent, what those who looked into them saw.
- **THE PALANTIR OF ORTHANC.** Possessed by Saruman, this stone was originally used for good. But as the white wizard increasingly sank into madness and evil, this palantir came increasingly under the domination of Sauron. In the end, it was appropriated by Aragorn and, by supreme effort, wrenched to his will.
- **THE PALANTIR OF MINAS TIRITH.** One of the seeing stones had been kept in the Tower of the Guard from time immemorial. Denethor, son of Ecthelion, began increasingly to use it during the period prior to the War of the Ring. Sauron, unable to break his will, was nonetheless able to control what he saw, sufficient to drive the steward of Gondor to madness and eventual suicide.

It's possible that Aragorn, at the end of the War of the Ring, was able to use the palantir to keep track of his friends as they returned to their separate homes in the West. It's more likely that it is of little use to him. Possibly he and Arwen can use it as a sort of Middle-earth-style big screen television. After all, he can't look into the palantir of Minas Tirith (it only shows two hands withering in fire); and he can't look at the palantir of Barad-dûr (it was destroyed during the collapse of the Dark Tower). What's he going to watch? ESPN?

Wizards' Staves

Well, it's not quite like Harry Potter (in which the wand chooses the wizard), but there does seem to be something similar going on in Middle-earth. After all, when Gandalf confronts Saruman in the ruins of Isengard, he tells him that he wants his staff and the Key of Orthanc. "They shall be pledges of your conduct, to be returned later, if you merit them." Also, apparently footwear is involved, since Saruman sneers, "Later, yes, when you have the keys of Barad-dûr itself, I suppose, and the crowns of seven kings and the rods of the Five Wizards and have purchased yourself a pair of boots many sizes larger than those you wear now!" Aside from what wizards wear for walking, what's the deal with their staves?

Gandalf himself relies on his staff during his confrontation with Wormtongue at Meduseld. Despite the best efforts of Théoden's counselor to keep it outside, Gandalf takes his staff into the Golden Hall and there works magic upon the enspelled king. During his confrontation with the balrog on the Bridge of Khazad-dûm, his staff is broken; presumably it's restored to him by the Lady Galadriel during his long healing in Lothlórien. (This point is never explained; I suppose Tolkien expected readers to work it out on our own.)

Wizards' staves are clearly key to their magic, and an enterprising hobbit (or anyone else) would be well advised to pay close attention to what these wise beings do with them.

Offensive Magic

Considering the number of fights that they get into, hobbits setting out on adventures would be smart to find someone or something capable of launching magical attacks on dangerous creatures such as goblins and wargs. In *The Hobbit*, the only person capable of doing so is Gandalf; the dwarves in the party are no help as far as magic is concerned. (Indeed, the dwarves of *The Hobbit* spend most of their time running away from danger rather than confronting it, and their ability to do so is usually the result of Bilbo or Gandalf's timely intervention.)

Fireballs

Common though these may be in other magical adventures, the use of fireballs in a hobbit's world is strictly limited. Perhaps it's because fireballs tend to kill everything and everyone around them when they explode, including enemies, friends, and innocent bystanders. If you have the capacity to unleash a fireball (and you probably don't unless you're a wizard), be sparing of them and use them only for emergencies. If, for instance, your dwarven companions are being interrogated by the Great Goblin while their ponies are being prepared for the goblin knackers, it's acceptable to launch a fireball that creates a diversion sounding like "several hundred dogs and cats being roasted alive."

Blasts

When Gandalf, the dwarves, and the hobbit are trapped in fifteen fir trees by a combined force of goblins and wolves, the wizard, in a last desperate blast of magic, prepares to come crashing down amid the goblins and wargs, taking as many of them as he can. He's providentially saved from going this course by the king of the eagles, who swoops down and grabs him. This is a good course for those bent on suicide. If you want to live a bit longer, you might want to think of a different plan.

Sheets of Fire

In moments of extreme tension, wizards can pull off some pretty spectacular special effects—George Lucas has nothing on Gandalf. Take, for instance, the moment when the balrog challenges the wizard on the Bridge of Khazad-dúm. Gandalf, crying aloud (presumably shouting out the words to a spell), hits the bridge in front of him with his staff, cracking and breaking both of them: the staff and the bridge. A "sheet of flame" flares up. That's bad news for the balrog, who realizes he's met his match.

BALROG FIGHTING TIP

The best kinds of spells to use when fighting a balrog are those that can be launched from a distance. Trying to have a sword fight on a narrow bridge over a bottomless chasm with a creature that's about ten times taller than you while trying to protect your friends who just want to get the hell out of there ... well, that probably won't end well, will it?

Fiery Trees

When the Fellowship is trapped on the top of a small hill by an attacking force of wolves, Gandalf solves the problem by setting the trees surrounding the hill on fire. It's hard to see how doing so is going to do any good—the wolves are quite equal to jumping between the tree trunks, and aside from giving the defenders better light to see, it doesn't really do anything to help—except it does. The wargs are frightened off by the spectacular display, the last arrow of Legolas ignites in the air before plunging into the heart of the wolf chieftain, and the rest of the night passes without incident. So the lesson here is, if you're threatened with an attack, set the wallpaper on fire. At the very least, it'll scare the hell out of your opponent.

A Light in the Dark

Gandalf, when push comes to shove, can produce light out of pretty much nothing. When the Fellowship enters the Mines of Moria, he produces a light at the end of his staff. As a wizard, you'd think he'd be able to do a bit more, but any light's a comfort as the party proceeds. For one thing, it stops them from falling into abandoned wells—as

Pippin and Merry almost do at one point. Gandalf's light, while not technically offensive, offers a guide to others.

Defensive Magic

The most obvious absence in the Fellowship, as any good role player will tell you, is a healer. That is to say, the group needs someone who can take care of battle-earned injuries quickly and efficiently, and without fainting at the sight of blood. Sam is probably the best naturally equipped to deal with this, but it's Aragorn who falls into the role, because he's king. This seems logical—a king heals the land as well as his subjects, and he relates to individuals as well as to the whole. Aragorn knows herb lore as well as battle smarts, and thus he's indicated as the true king of Gondor. The lesson? Anyone who's as well rounded as Aragorn and as good-looking as Viggo Mortensen is probably good at healing as well as hurting. At any rate, there are an awful lot of women who'd like to let him try.

Healing Magic

Some magic works to heal wounds, whether physical or psychic. In any circumstance in which you might be groping for a band-aid, consider instead trying a healing spell. Of course, it helps if you're an elf (their race excels in such magic) or a Númenórean king (since the hands of the king are the hands of a healer, as Ioreth of Minas Tirith never ceases to say). In any case, if you're attempting to heal someone of wounds taken in battle, here are some guidelines.

Athelas Is Pretty Much Good for Anything

It's also called kingsfoil, asea aronian, and probably some other names. It grows widely and in different climates. Aragorn finds it first in the north to treat Frodo and then in the south to heal Faramir. Whatever the case, it is remarkably simple in its preparation:

1. Cut some fresh athelas—a bunchful should do the trick in the case of most wounds.
2. Crush several leaves and rub them together.
3. Breathe deeply to impress those around you.
4. Throw the leaves into bowls of steaming (but not boiling) water and let the steam waft through the room.
5. Tell everyone how much better they feel. Repeat as necessary.

Athelas is considered a common herb and is handy for use with many wounds and ailments: orc spear stab wounds, Morgul knife wounds, exposure to the Black Breath, and just general depression brought on by the Dark Lord and his powers.

Don't be Afraid to Use Splints

Just because you're living in a fantasy world doesn't mean old-fashioned medical methods aren't going to work. If someone breaks an arm, tie it up tightly in a rigid position and fasten it with a branch or stick so it doesn't move. Slings are useful to support injured limbs. So are miscellaneous bandages, especially for those who've been wounded in the head while slaying forty-two orcs.

Magical Therapy 101

In the case of those who may have succumbed to evil magic (and there's a lot of that floating around), restorative is indicated. Wizards can perform spells to break evil spirit possession, and the elves are always available to heal the tortured soul, if not through magic directly, then through the long healing arts of the Undying Lands.

Magical Artifacts

We've already touched on the palantiri, wrought by Feanor in the depths of the Second Age. Hobbits and their kin are well advised to stay away from objects so powerful. Likewise, there's no good reason to mess around with the Rings of Power, wizards' staves, or any of the most ominous magical artifacts that are strewn through Middle-earth.

Galadriel's Mirror

Sam, naively, asks to see some elf magic, and Galadriel obliges with the mirror. Who wouldn't want to see a magical mirror that tells the future? It's a very old fantasy trope: the magical mirror from Snow White, the mirror that tells Beauty that her father is dying and she must leave the Beast to save him. The list goes on and on.

Galadriel's mirror differs in two ways:

1. She creates the mirror from water, which means its surface is highly changeable and transient.
2. She warns both Sam and Frodo that the mirror is unreliable. Most other mirror users don't acknowledge this fact. Snow White's wicked queen completely believes the mirror on the wall when it says she's not the fairest one of all.

The mirror of Galadriel seems to be an artifact that's bound to her own magical powers; that is to say, it can't appear without her. Presumably we'd be able to see and use the mirror from Snow White, if we could get the wicked queen away from it for five minutes.

The Mere of Khazad-Dûm

After the Fellowship of the Ring's horrible experience's in Moria, including the loss of their leader, a centuries-old wizard who was the only one with a clear idea of how to accomplish the quest of Mount Doom, Gimli's idea is naturally to take Frodo to look at the Mirror-mere. I mean, what else would you do after a disaster of such epic proportions? As it turns out, it's a spiritual experience for both Frodo and for Sam, who tags along, as usual, uninvited. All Frodo and Sam see when they look in the Mere is a circle of stars, like a crown, encircling the mountains, and no sign of their own reflections. On the whole, the Mirrormere is pretty disappointing, making Galadriel's mirror appear even more impressive.

The Phial of Galadriel

For someone with the perception of a five thousand-year-old elf princess/queen, you'd think she'd be better at giving momentous gifts. She gives Frodo Baggins an incredibly important, valuable gift at the crucial stage of his quest ("it stands upon a knife blade") and doesn't explain how to use it. Fortunately for him, he has some instincts in the matter, realizing that when you wield magical elf objects, the best thing is to accompany them with magical elf words such as Elbereth Githoniel. This works in the lair of Shelob, again in the tower of Cirith Ungol, but not so much in the depths of Mount Doom. Later in the story, Frodo gives Sting to Sam, as well as his suit of elf mail, which he got from Bilbo. But he never explains what he did with the Phial of Galadriel, which Sam faithfully carried for him in Mordor. Could it be that Frodo takes it with him to the Undying Lands? (Where, one would think, it would be sort of pointless.)

The Rings of Power

We know, in the end, that Elrond held Vilya, the most important of the three elven rings; Gandalf held Narya the Great; and Galadriel held Nenya, a ring created of *mithril* which Frodo and Sam saw for the first time in Lothlórien (Sam actually thought it was a star seen through Galadriel's fingers). With the three elven rings, we approach the essence of magical power in Middle-earth. With these rings, the three mightiest magical figures of the age created and maintained the world. The lesson for those of hobbit persuasion setting off on adventure seems clear: Make friends with Ringbearers. Good things come to those who are loyal and see adventures through to the end. In fact, in the case of Samwise Gamgee, bearing a ring for a while guarantees the possibility of leaving the Grey Havens and traveling over the Sundering Seas to the Undying Lands. And that's not a bad reward for a life well lived.

The Cracks of Doom

Well, okay. The Cracks of Doom, in the middle of Mount Doom, are a really evil, crappy place to wind up, especially after weeks of traveling on limited rations and practically no water. We get that. But the Cracks are also the ancient forges of Sauron. Really? Seriously? How does he do it? How does he create the most powerful magical artifacts in the history of Middle-earth out of a couple of chasms in a mountain tunnel? In point of fact, Sauron has magical powers that are centered on the Cracks of Doom and the Ring, and it doesn't do anyone any good to mess with them.

(Dagical Beings

If you're setting off on an adventure, you can certainly expect to encounter magical creatures of varying powers and attitudes. These range from the ordinary (elves) to the surprising (trolls) to the epic (Ringwraiths). The average adventurer, in order to live a comfortable life, should be prepared to deal with each of these.

Elves

By the time certain hobbits start having adventures, elves have become relatively rare—almost as rare as dwarves and hobbits. Most of them are leaving Middle-earth, on their way to the West, and they aren't interested in being bothered. Elves are a bit like the French: They once had a great empire, are still unreasonably proud of it, and don't care to talk about what happened to it. They enjoy a lot of magic, more than most other races of Middle-earth, but it's not very helpful in the day-to-day.

Dwarves

Dwarves possess very little magic, partly it would seem from living so physically close to the earth. Still, no one is better at getting a fire started, even in rainy weather, and that's pretty magical. Dwarves are also good at finding their way about underground and at fixing broken stonework. These are some excellent talents that others should emulate.

Men

The men of Númenor are about the only magical figures left among men. Besides being long-lived, they remember ancient magic from the days of Númenor and Gondolin. Aragorn, however, throughout *The Lord of the Rings*, comes across as singularly unmagical. Bard of Lake-town, on the other hand, understands the languages of thrushes, a language that gives him a considerable advantage in the battle with Smaug.

Hobbits

Hobbits are about the least magical race one can imagine. Though in *The Hobbit* it's said that they boast "ordinary magic" that allows them to vanish when the "Big People" come blundering along, we're also told that their abilities to vanish are actually just a highly developed hiding capacity "so that to humans it may look magical." As a rule, hobbits don't like magic very much, unless it's the kind used at a child's birthday party.

Ask yourself the following questions to determine which of Middle-earth's races you most resemble:

    1. When confronted by a dangerous situation do you:

        a. roll up your sleeves and prepare for battle

        b. think back on the long line of your ancestors who fought evil and compose an epic poem about it

        c. take a deep draft of mead, sharpen your axe, and smile

       d. lock the door, turn up the light, and go to bed with some extra covers.

2. If you could obtain a chest of gold, you'd:
   a. say, "Great!" and start spending your newfound money
   b. reject gold, since you're above money
   c. bury the gold safely, with many spells and enchantments, so you can come back and retrieve it at a future date
   d. ignore it. It's probably Evil Enchanted Gold anyway.

3. In talking to a dragon, you'd probably:
   a. be constantly thinking about soft points, as well as how to get away so I can relay that information to others
   b. wouldn't say anything; why would I be talking to anything like a dragon anyway?
   c. be very clever, ferreting out as much information about the beast's hoard as possible, or
   d. Dragon? What dragon? I see no dragon. After all, if I can't see it, it can't see me.

If you answered mostly:

       a. You're human.

       b. You're an elf. An annoying elf.

       c. You're a dwarf.

       d. You're a hobbit. If there's an adventure, you'd prefer to be left out of it.

Good Wizard or Bad Wizard

There are five wizards in Middle-earth (Gandalf the Grey; Saruman the White; Radagast the Brown; and two others unnamed, whom Tolkien mentioned in later correspondence as "Blue"). Saruman is evil in the latter part of his life, and Gandalf is "the enemy of Sauron"—in other words, the epitome of good. However, it's not always easy to tell a good wizard from a bad wizard.

To determine whether a wizard is bad or good, uncover their opinions on the following questions:

1. Are men hopelessly corrupt and weak, and do they require a strong hand to guide them and keep them from getting into trouble?

2. In the interest of the Greater Good, is it okay to sacrifice numerous members of lesser races (including Ents, elves, and hobbits)?

3. Is the most important thing in the world:
   a. order
   b. security
   c. an almost fanatical devotion to our lord and master Sauron the Great
   d. the peace and happiness of the races of the West

4. In securing the safety of the peoples of Middle-earth, would you be prepared to:
   a. enslave them
   b. help someone else enslave them
   c. take on the burden of bearing the One Ring, though it would be a tremendous personal sacrifice
   d. sacrifice your own safety and comfort?

5. Elves are:
   a. an annoyance
   b. an anachronism
   c. food
   d. the bearers of ancient wisdom.

If the wizard answers "yes" to the first two questions and anything but (d) to the remaining four, run. Run fast.

One of the confusing things about wizards is that they tend to look alike. Gandalf and Saruman, for instance, are both old men who wear robes of white (although Saruman's robe isn't really white, if you look at it closely enough; it shimmers and seems to incorporate all color). You cannot trust appearance alone, so probe deeper. For example:

- If the wizard is riding on a shining white horse and is followed by an army of animate trees, he's good.
- If the wizard is ragged, unkempt, and clinging to a tobacco pouch with the monogram "M.B.", he's bad.
- If the wizard is riding on the back of an eagle, he's good.
- If the wizard is slinking around the edges of a forest, he's bad.
- If the wizard is in command of a giant army of orcs and wargs laying waste to everything they see, he's bad. Stay out of his way.

Wizards are ancient spirits of Middle-earth (called "Maiar"). What other creatures encountered in Tolkien's works are Maiar in a different form?

      a. Elves

      b. Hobbits

      c. Balrogs

      d. Dragons

      e. Orc chieftains

The answer is c, balrogs.

Don't Make a Wizard Angry

Wizards are notoriously short-tempered. It's easy to tell when a wizard is angry, because he starts growling, his eyebrows bristle, he stops answering questions, and he gives short, sharp puffs on his pipe. He also stops blowing smoke rings and becomes snappish. On the other hand, a happy wizard laughs, plays practical jokes on his friends, and eats and drinks a lot. Especially drinks. A lot.

The Magic of Wizards

Every wizard has his own special type of magic. Gandalf's, for instance, is fire based: He can create fire from pretty much nothing; his fireworks are legendary; and he can set treetops on fire to repel an attack by magical wolves. Saruman, on the other hand, in his latter, evil phase, can corrupt the hearts of men using his voice. Even when Saruman's powers have been largely taken away from him and his staff is broken, his voice can still move men—and hobbits—to evil. Radagast is a master of shapes and hues and can talk to birds and beasts. So the wise hobbit will learn to use all the strengths and weaknesses of wizards, and avoid irritating them unnecessarily.

Elf Magic

Aside from the magic displayed by Galadriel's mirror for the benefit of Frodo and Sam, there's not much elf magic on offer in Middle-earth. That is, unless you look a little closer. Elves have an inherent magical quality; after all, they're immortal beings, blessed by the Valar, which makes them magical to begin with. Those places most infested with elves acquire a magical quality that lingers long after the elves have gone. The enterprising adventurer will seek out these places and benefit from the remnants of magical power there.

Lothlórien

This is, perhaps, the most magical place in all of Middle-earth: the Golden Wood, ruled by Galadriel and her consort, Celeborn. Outsiders can perceive the power there, and it's viewed with great concern by Sauron, but he can do nothing directly to combat it. (Lothlórien is, effectively, the counterpart of Dol Guldur, Sauron's former fastness in southern Mirkwood.) Should an adventurer visit Lothlórien, he will find his hurts healed and his spirit renewed. He'll also spend a lot more time there than he bargained for, since time flows very quickly and slowly in this land. What might seem a few weeks will turn out to be several months. If you have an urgent errand to carry out, Lothlórien might be a good place to avoid. However, if you want to view the heart of elfdom in Middle-earth, this is the place to go.

Post-Galadriel Lothlórien

When Galadriel leaves Middle-earth on the same boat that carries Gandalf, Bilbo, and Frodo, much of the magic leaves the Golden Wood, though Celeborn stays there for a while. Places such as Lothlórien are few and far between, but the magic in them is so strong that even today you can find it in remote wooded glades and the depths of primeval forests.

Mirkwood

If you happen to stray into Mirkwood the Great, be advised not to leave the path to chase will-o'-the-wisp lights. If you're searching for the elves who inhabit this great forest, don't worry, they'll find you first. Elves in this forbidding wood often feast in the forest, especially in the late autumn. Outsiders definitely aren't welcome and are likely to find themselves wandering in the dark, bumping into spiders if they try to interrupt an elven feast. The lesson is: Wait for an invitation. If the elves want to talk to you, they'll find a way. After all, you're on their turf now.

Elf Gifts

If, by chance, you're lucky enough to spend some time with the elves, these gracious hosts may give you some very handy parting gifts. Treasure them. Some examples:

- A scabbard for your sword that ensures your sword won't ever be broken or tarnished. That's got to be good.
- A box of magical dust that enables you to grow a garden in record time.
- A vial containing pure light, which you can shine in moments of despair and darkness (until you get really close to the enemy, in which case the vial becomes useless).
- Some hairs from the head of an elf queen. They'll be useful for ... well, I'm sure they'll be helpful at some point.
- Belts. They keep your trousers up when you haven't eaten a decent meal in weeks.

Dwarf Magic

Dwarves aren't a particularly magical race; most of their magic is devoted to finding their way around dark mines and tunnels and delving for precious stones and metals. Not that such things aren't useful—it's just that dwarves aren't obviously magical the way that elves are, the big show-offs!

If you want to see some dwarf magic, go to one of the following places.

The Bridge of Khazad-dûm

Strictly speaking, this is more a feat of engineering than of magic. A single span of stone, jumping more than fifty feet over a bottomless chasm. It has no rails and is very narrow, allowing trespassers into the underground realm to cross only in single file (and be picked off by dwarf archers on the far side). However, we might pause to ask how such a bridge could possibly support the weight of dwarves, elves, humans, hobbits, and in an extreme case, a balrog. The answer seems pretty clearly to be magic, especially when Gandalf, fighting the balrog, uses magic to break the bridge. If the dwarves, after returning to Moria upon the defeat of Sauron, rebuilt the bridge, visiting it is certainly an adventure to put on your bucket list.

The Mirrormere

We mentioned this earlier. Not, perhaps, the most exciting place, but if you're doing a tour of Dwarf Magical Sites, it's not to be missed.

The Lonely Mountain

Again, this is less about magic than about a famous site of a magical battle. It was the refuge of Smaug after he smoked out the dwarves and took over their kingdom. And it was also the location of the Battle of Five Armies, fought between elves, dwarves, men, orcs, and wargs. Gandalf, who was present at the battle, seems to have refrained from any last-minute blasts of magic, but there's probably plenty of magical energy lingering on the surrounding countryside. After the battle, the mountain became the site of a dwarf kingdom, ruled by Dáin Ironfoot (eventually killed in battle with Sauron's forces during an outlying battle of the War of the Ring), and there are plenty of things to see and do if you care to visit there.

Miscellaneous Magical Sites

Middle-earth has plenty of magic for anyone who looks for it. So does the rest of the world, for that matter. The trick is to look in the right places. Places that have been the sites of great battles. Places that are associated with ancient artifacts. Places that have been the location of great evil or good. Among such places in Middle-earth, we mustn't leave out the following.

Weathertop

Once the great fortress of Amon-sul, this is now a sad, lonely ruin on a mountaintop that surveys the surrounding countryside. It was the site of an epic confrontation between the Ringwraiths and Frodo and Aragorn, and some of the old magic lingers. Anyone trying to reach Rivendell won't want to pass this mountain without climbing it and, perhaps, spending a night in the dell below the peak.

Meduseld

The Golden Hall, foundation of the nation of Rohan, and former seat of Théoden, son of Thengel (and later the seat of Eomer, son of Eomund). What little magic the Riders of Rohan have is centered on horses, their first love. In the Golden Hall, you'll find many tributes to the close bond that exists between the people of Rohan and their steeds, including the mearas, the greatest horses in all Middle-earth. Generally, alert and enterprising adventurers can talk to or at least understand the speech of most animals. This is especially true of the Riders of Rohan and their horses. The skill may not be technically magical, but it's extremely useful in battle.

Isengard

The fortress of Saruman was largely destroyed by Ents during the War of the Ring, but they couldn't damage the tower of Isengard itself, which is certainly magical and designed to withstand any assault, magic or otherwise. Isengard consists of a large rock ring, within which are avenues leading to the tower at the center. This, in turn, divides into two towers as it rises, and between the towers at the top is a narrow platform, inscribed with mystic symbols, the sort of thing wizards like to meditate on. Below, there are all sorts of tunnels and caverns, probably reeking with magic, though not the sort of magic you'd care to mess with. The keys of Orthanc (another name for Isengard) are in the care of the king of Gondor.

Appendix A

A Dragon's Perspective

We've spent time discussing the hobbit approach to life—an approach that is innocent, humble, and well mannered. As with anything in life, it may be helpful to consider an alternative point of view. For that, who better to turn to than a dragon, chief villain of *The Hobbit* and creature of myth and legend? If one could have a discussion with a worm, what might he say? What thoughts might the fearsome creature have about life, about hobbits, and about the human world? We thought it would be fun to find out in an interview.

Hello, kind Dragon. Thanks for taking the time to talk to us today.

Who are you and why are you here? Do you not know to whom you speak? Do you wish to perish in flame? What is the meaning of this intrusion?

Apologies, O Tremendous Dragon. We only want to witness your greatness, that we may see it for ourselves.

Well. It seems you know of me ... [yawns] I suppose I will allow you audience. What is it you seek? This isn't about my treasure, is it? Touch the treasure and you're toast.

Toast?

Ah, well, it is the age of men, now, isn't it? One must keep up with the common vernacular.

O Mighty Dragon, would you, in your magnificence, see fit to entertain a few questions?

I suppose, but first answer mine or suffer my fearsome wrath. Who are you and from whence did you come?

We are but the Pen-wielders, the Page-fillers, the Word-benders who've come to chronicle your exaltedness. We come from the Shire ... by way of Cincinnati.

Fancy titles! But words will only take you so far. Watch your tongue or you'll be bathed in fire.

Um ... let's talk about you.

Oh, very well. I've counted my treasure more times than I can remember, so why not? Get on with it, O illustrious Word-bender.

O Resplendent Dragon...

Careful Pen-wielder. Do you want to burn?

No, not today, thank you all the same.

Well ... get on with it.

Ah ... yes ... well, what is your chief pleasure in life, O Devine Dragon?

That's your question? Really, Page-filler? Do you not see this mound of treasure I perch upon? This cradle of gold and jewels? This chaise of riches? This divan of wealth? This is the kind of treasure they write about in *Forbes*. Need you ask what it is that brings me pleasure?

Well, yes. But what do you do with it?

What do you mean, "What do I do with it?" I own it. What kind of silly question is that? "What do I do with it?" Really. What's your next question, fool?

How do you come by so much wealth, O Wise and Fearsome Dragon?

Oh, now that's a much better question. I pillage, of course—and that is the real fun, you see. I soar high above your pathetic little towns, my awesome wings darkening your skies. (See how big and magnificent they are?) [spreads awesome wings] And when I see something that sparkles, I swoop down raining fire and destruction upon everything in my path until I clutch the trinket in my sharp, sharp talon. (See how sharp it is? Would you like to test it, Word-bender?).

So the treasure's not really yours?

Of course it's mine! Who else would it belong to? Anyone who might lay claim to it is but a cinder. Either that, or their bones filled my belly for a time.

I ... um ... believe I see a few artifacts that may have once belonged to dwarves.

Speak to me not of dwarves. Have you ever tasted a dwarf? Tough, gristly, gamey creatures. Believe you me, after a meal of dwarves, one deserves a pile of treasure.

What about hobbits?

Hobbits? What's that?

You know, a hobbit ... a halfling. They make great burglars.

A hobbit. You know, I think I met one once. Filthy bugger crept into my lair and stole a golden cup from me. He was, however, very polite about it. He paid me all sorts of compliments and seemed truly impressed by my fine scales. Come to think of it, he sounded a bit like you.

O Dazzling and Radiant Dragon, what can you tell us about today's world?

Today's world? You want a dragon's opinion about the age of men? An age when wealth is transferred over the computer and no one keeps vaults filled with actual gold and jewels to lie about in? An age where buildings are all made of metal and concrete and flame retardant materials?

Truly, your Impressiveness.

Well, first of all, there's not much to eat. Men used to be quite tasty—a much more satisfying morsel than, say, a dwarf. But, alas, today men taste of chemicals. I imagine it's all the Coke Zeros and Dorito tacos. They can't be good for you. Can you imagine a dragon with an ulcer? Talk about heartburn. It's an absolute travesty.

But I guess there are some things I like about today's world. The phones keep getting shinier and shinier—I wouldn't mind having a pile of those to lie in. I like Words With Friends. Oh, and stretch Hummers crack me up. Global warming keeps things nice and balmy. And if the oil companies keep up the good work, pretty soon I'll be able to set all of the oceans on fire.

O Really Cool Dragon—

Now, what are you carrying on about?

I'm trying to employ the common vernacular, just like you said....

And that's the best you can do? Really Word-bender, you're beginning to test my patience. My teeth are like javelins, my claws like daggers, and my breath a raging inferno.

O Dragon the Totally Rad?

Shall I smite you? I'm starting to think you want me to.

What are your thoughts on friendship and love?

I eat ponies for breakfast.

Is there any good in the world, O Brilliant Dragon?

Is this some kind of hobbit thing? Because, seriously. Dwarves are greedy creatures, grubbing for gold and treasure at every turn. Elves are a bunch of weirdos off somewhere dancing in the forest half the time. And men? Don't get me started. Men are easily corrupted, killing one another over the smallest of quibbles. And here you are asking me about goodness and love. Did you miss the part where I'M A DRAGON? Thunderous wings, tail like a tree trunk, monstrous talons?

O Resplendent Drag...

Frrrrroooooom. [A curtain of flame sadly concludes our interview.]

Appendix B

Hobbit Words and
Their Human Equivalents

ATTERCOP: Another name for a spider (derogatory connotation).

ATHELAS: Also known as kingsfoil, this is an herb of Middle-earth known for its healing properties. It's the Middle-earth equivalent of Neosporin, aspirin, and chicken noodle soup all rolled into one.

BALROG: Fiery demonic beings of Middle-earth, often armed with flaming whips. Bad news no matter if you live in Middle-earth or the "real" world... a demon's a demon.

BANNOCKS: A flat cake typically cooked on a griddle. Yep, they're pancakes.

BATTLE OF THE FIVE ARMIES: This final battle depicted in *The Hobbit* was a fight waged by armies of men, elves, dwarves and eagles against the goblins and wargs. The whole thing started with the men and elves arguing with the dwarves over claims to Smaug's treasure. The next thing you know all of them come under the attack of goblins riding giant wolves. The best modern-day comparison is a typical Thanksgiving dinner with extended family.

THE BLACK BREATH: A serious medical condition caused by contact with a Ringwraith. It's like getting "the cooties" from an unpopular kid in grade school you, only it's real and more like The Plague.

BOWLS: A hobbit game similar to bowling.

BURGLAR: In Middle-earth, a burglar is a treasure hunter who uses stealth in order to avoid dangerous situations. In human culture, the word has a negative connotation, generally meaning *thief*. Even in Middle-earth the term *burglar* is rather distasteful to hobbits because of their aversion to adventure.

CAVE TROLLS: A breed of trolls specialized for dwelling in tunnels and caverns.

CONEY: Another word for a rabbit.

CRAM: A type of dwarven bread used in Middle-earth for long travels. Similar to hardtack, which is a type of biscuit or cracker that has a long shelf life and was often used by sailors or the military. *Cram* is the cause of many broken teeth.

DWARVES: Dwarves are short, hardworking folk. Typically miners by trade, dwarves are experts at hard work such as digging and building. In human culture, dwarves would be tradesmen—contractors, carpenters, plumbers, and the like. Useful people to have around, dwarves.

ELVES: The elves of Middle-earth are wise and beautiful beings. The elves hold the secrets of the West, are immortal, and generally have their shit together. In human culture, elves would be the celebrities, models, rock stars, and the Hollywood elite—the in-crowd, so to speak.

ENTS: An ancient race of anthropomorphic treelike creatures who dwell in the forests of Middle-earth. They are patient and cautious. They take their time to make a decision about anything. In your day-to-day life, dealings with hippies or granolas might be similar to conversing with Ents.

FALLOHIDES: A subrace of hobbits who are tall (for hobbits) and fair-haired with a light complexion. In today's world, Fallohides would be the hobbit elite (as far as that goes for hobbits, which is nothing compared to elves).

FAUNT: A young hobbit (two to five years in age). A faunt is the hobbit equivalent of a toddler.

FELLOWSHIP: A fellowship is generally a group of friends or allies who band together in support of a common cause. They swear oaths and make lofty rallying speaches. Today's equivalent of a fellowship would likely be an LLC or a group of shareholders.

GOBLINS: Violent creatures who live in dark places, often underground. In human culture, goblins would likely be criminals who live in the sewers and subway tunnels. Also see "Orcs."

HALFLING: Another term for a hobbit. The term is in reference to their size, which is roughly half the size of humans. It's not recommended to use this term in human culture to refer to anyone, no matter their size, as it would likely be offensive.

HALFLING'S LEAF: A slang term for pipeweed, the tobacco cultivated by hobbits.

HARFOOTS: A subrace of hobbits who are the smallest in stature of the hobbits. Not that there's anything wrong with that.

HELM'S DEEP: The site of one of the largest and most important battles in *The Lord of the Rings*. Not to be mistaken for a typical Saturday at your local grocery store.

HOBGOBLINS: In Middle-earth a hobgoblin may refer to a larger and stronger breed of goblin or orc. See also "Uruk-hai."

HOBBIT HOLE: This refers to a hobbit's home—usually a comfortable home built into the side of a hill. Hobbit holes are quite cozy and well furnished. In human culture, many energy-efficient homes, such as adobe houses, are similar in idea to the hobbit-hole.

IMP: The offspring of a creature such as a goblin or an orc. In the human world, imps can often been found running unsupervised through your local International House of Pancakes.

KINGSFOIL: A healing herb. See Athelas.

LEMBAS: An elven bread, similar to hardtack or the dwarves' *cram*, only tastier and more nutritious. As you know from comparing short-bread cookies to the fudge stripe variety, elves can make anything taste better.

LONGBOTTOM LEAF: A variety of pipeweed grown in a region of the Shire known as Longbottom.

MATHOMS: A hobbit word for a regifted gift. Did you ever play the holiday gift exchange game where you keep selecting gifts until no one ends up with what they wanted, and then everyone takes it to the next holiday party they have to go to? It's pretty much exactly that.

MINCE-PIES: Hobbits are fond of hearty food such as these pies filled with chopped meat. In today's harried world, a chicken potpie might be a fair comparison.

MITHRIL: An incredibly strong lightweight material often made into chain mail armor. *Mithril* is like the Kevlar of Middle-earth.

MOON LETTERS: Elvish runes that can be seen only when the moon shines upon them. A human equivalent might be writing something in invisible ink to be decoded with lemon juice.

MORDOR: As the dwelling place of the Dark Lord Sauron, Mordor is a barren land covered with rock, ash and little vegetation. It's a hive of villainy, debauchery, and lies. Imagine if you combined Las Vegas, Washington D.C., and Hell into one and then threw in a couple of volcanoes. The result would be Mordor.

NAZGUL: Also known as Ringwraiths. These were men who succumbed to the power of the Dark Lord Sauron when presented with Rings of Power. The rings corrupted their minds and they became obsessed with attaining the one true ring. Today one might akin the Nazgul to politicians in a primary race, blindly seeking a seat of power, speaking lies, and making frightening desperate attempts to grasp a power they shouldn't be allowed to wield.

NECROMANCER: A dark wizard. One who practices dark arts. The modern-day human equivalent is probably a CEO of a technology company.

NINEPINS: A hobbit game similar to bowling.

NÚMENÓREANS: Men from a distant land who introduced tobacco to the hobbits. Today men who peddle tobacco are still targeting little people (first hobbits, now tweens and teens) in an attempt to get them hooked on the nasty habit. Some things never change.

OLD TOBY: A variety of pipeweed.

OGRES: Monsterous giants who are fond of feasting on flesh. Today's ogres prefer combo meals from drive-through windows.

ORCS: Similar to goblins, orcs are large violent creatures. In human culture you might think of orcs as street thugs who travel in groups looking for victims.

PALANTIRI: These are magical "seeing stones" of Middle-earth. Similar to a crystal ball, they are used to see other parts of the world or to communicate with (or influence) those who also have a palantiri. Today we accomplish the same thing with Skype.

QUOITS: A hobbit game similar to horseshoes or cornhole.

RANGERS: Men who patrolled the wilderness armed with swords, spears, and bows. They typically wore earth tones and dark cloaks. Today you can still find Rangers at your local renaissance fair.

RINGS OF POWER: Magical rings created by Sauron and gifted to Elves, Dwarves and Men with One Ring with the power to rule all others. These gifts of power tempted the wearers and brought the races of Middle-earth under the throng of Sauron. At first the rings seemed good and were able to do really cool things, but eventually they began to corrupt anyone who used them, driving them to obsession and insanity. You know, kind of like a smart phone.

RINGWRAITHS: Men driven insane under the throng of the rings of power. Also known as the Nazgul.

RIVENDALE: An Elf community often thought to be the most hospitable and wonderful place in Middle-earth. Kind of like a Middle-earth Disney World. Only maybe without the rides. Or the long lines.

SEED-CAKE: A dense cake of bread with one or more varieties of seeds baked into it. Today's equivalent might be an "everything" bagel.

SHIRE, THE: The Shire is home to the hobbits. More than just a place to live, the Shire is a place of significance. Think of your own childhood home, or a special place where you felt most relaxed and comfortable, and you'll have an idea of how the hobbits regard the Shire. We should all be so lucky as to live in such a place.

SKIN-CHANGER: A person who can turn into another creature, such as a bear. In *The Hobbit*, Bilbo and the dwarves are allowed to stay with Beorn, a skin-changer who shows his guests hospitality in return for hearing their tale of adventure. Today people might think of a skin-changer as a were-creature (such as a werewolf, or the Native American skin-walker).

SOUTHERN STAR: A variety of pipeweed.

STONE GIANTS: Large, unintellegent creatures that hurl massive stones at one another for fun. Stone giants today would likely be pro wrestlers.

STONE TROLLS: A breed of trolls that turn to stone in direct sunlight. Unfortunately this probably doesn't apply to the trolls you know.

STOORS: A subrace of hobbits who are stocky and broad chested. In today's world, Stoors would be considered the blue-collar class of hobbits.

TOMNODDY: A foolish being. The equivalent of calling someone a "big dummy.".

TROLLS: Trolls are large, dull creatures. They have plenty of physical strength but aren't very clever. They are typically crude and loud. In human culture they aren't much different. You've probably met your share of trolls in noisy pubs, at sporting events, or on their smart-phones at the movies.

THE UNDYING LANDS: This is a sort of promised land for elves where they would spend their immortal lives, usually after already having lived a long life in Middle-earth. It's like a retirement community for elves.

URUK-HAI: An advanced breed of orcs or goblins. If orcs are the thugs of MiddleEarth, you might think of the Uruk-hai as a well-organized street gang.

VIOLS: Stringed musical instruments, similar to violins.

WARGS: Large wolves that are sometimes ridden by orcs or goblins.

WATER-SKIN: A leather bag made to hold water—the Middle-earth equivalent of a water bottle or canteen.

WIGHTS: Wraiths or ghostlike creatures of Middle-earth.

WORM: (Also Wyrm). Another word for *dragon* (derogatory).

Don't let your journey through Middle-earth end here

The Unofficial Hobbit Trivia Challenge

BY NICK HURWITCH

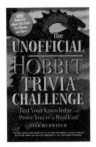

You may think that you know everything there is to know about Bilbo, the Shire, and Middle-earth, but how much do you really know? With topics ranging from the lore of dragons, elves, dwarves, and other inhabitants of Tolkien's world to the directors, writers, and artists he inspired, you can find out if you're a real fan of the greatest imaginary world ever created.

Dictionary of Made-up Languages

BY COLIN DURIEZ

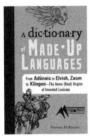

Can you converse in Klingon? Ask an Elf the time of day? Greet a speaker of Esperanto? These are among the more than 100 constructed languages you'll find in this book. For each one, author Stephen D. Rogers provides vocabulary, grammatical features, background information on the language and its inventor, and fascinating facts.

Available from AdamsMediaStore.com and your favorite book retailers.

The Unofficial HOBBIT HANDBOOK

WD
WRITER'S DIGEST BOOKS
WritersDigest.com
Cincinnati, Ohio

Everything I Need to Know About Life I Learned From Tolkien

The Shire Collective

For more resources for writers, visit www.writersdigest.com/books.

To receive a free weekly e-mail newsletter delivering tips and updates about writing and about Writer's Digest products, register directly at http://newsletters.fwpublications.com.

10 9 8 7 6 5 4 3 2 1

Distributed in Canada by Fraser Direct
100 Armstrong Avenue
Georgetown, Ontario, Canada L7G 5S4
Tel: (905) 877-4411

Distributed in the U.K. and Europe by F&W Media International
Brunel House, Newton Abbot, Devon, TQ12 4PU, England
Tel: (+44) 1626-323200, Fax: (+44) 1626-323319
E-mail: enquiries@fwmedia.com

Distributed in Australia by Capricorn Link
P.O. Box 704, Windsor, NSW 2756 Australia
Tel: (02) 4577-3555

Edited by Rachel Scheller
Designed by Claudean Wheeler
Illustrations by Ben Patrick
Production coordinated by Debbie Thomas